PREACHING

PREACHING

By
G. CAMPBELL MORGAN

EDITED BY KURT I. JOHANSON
FOREWORD BY TIMOTHY S. WARREN
AFTERWORD BY PETER VERKRUYSE

WIPF & STOCK · Eugene, Oregon

Wipf and Stock Publishers
199 W 8th Ave, Suite 3
Eugene, OR 97401

Preaching
By Morgan, G. Campbell and Johanson, Kurt I.
Copyright©1937 by Morgan, G. Campbell
ISBN 13: 978-1-5326-4843-4
Publication date 7/16/2018
Previously published by Baker Book House, 1974

FOREWORD TO THE 2018 EDITION

EIGHTY YEARS have transpired since the first publication of G. Campbell Morgan's influential *Preaching*. Our world has experienced unprecedented and unimaginable change during those eight decades. Yet, the Word of God and the need of man have remained constant. Those who rebel against the authority and holiness of God stagger under the burden of sin's consequences. At the same time, divine grace still invites sinners into eternal fellowship with God through faith in the Lord Jesus Christ. Morgan's own definition of preaching as "the declaration of the grace of God to human need on the authority of the Throne of God, [demanding] on the part of those who hear that they show obedience to the thing declared" faithfully identifies the essence of all true preaching. Because these most basic truths remain changeless, and since Morgan addressed the topic of preaching at that most basic level, this reprinting of *Preaching* will faithfully guide another generation through the principles of proclaiming the message of the Bible to meet the need of mankind.

The value of Morgan's slim volume results from the thoughtful discipline of his organized mind. He had a method. That method was not complex, though it was demanding. Morgan prescribed five distinct steps in the preparation of a sermon. First, Survey: the text must be read, in its context, at least forty and as many as fifty times. The "context" included the entire book in which the passage was found. The goal was to catch a bird's-eye or telescopic view of the biblical author's message. Second, Condense: the broad outline of the text must be written out. This overview of the main points should synthesize both the book and the chapter or verse under consideration. Third, Expand: a more exhaustive outline must be expressed, in terms of sub-points, in order to fill out the author's development. Fourth, Dissect: the text must be studied for all its detail, providing a microscopic view of the text in support of the preceding outlines. Fifth: Consult: the work of other scholars should certainly be considered, but only after the preacher has completed his own systematic study.

G. Campbell Morgan practiced that method throughout seven decades of fruitful ministry in Great Britain, France, the United States, and Canada. *Preaching* develops several practical, yet essential, strategies for implementing that method. Every Bible teacher and preacher will want to know and practice more than what is found in these ninety pages, but every faithful Bible teacher and preacher must know and practice at least what is contained in this book. Morgan's systematic method and practical strategies have proven timeless. He still speaks for the benefit of twenty-first century preachers.

G. Campbell Morgan was born on December 9, 1863, in the village of Tetbury, England. Although his great-grandfather had been yeoman farmer and his grandfather a shepherd, his father was a Baptist preacher, with Brethren leanings. Young Morgan was educated at home by his strict father and a tutor, and received more formal teaching at Gratton House. Though he never earned a degree, Morgan was self-taught well beyond what a university education could have provided.

Young George "played at preaching" as early as age six and was encouraged in that direction when in 1873 he heard D. L. Moody preach. He preached his first official sermon at Monmouth Methodist Church on August 27, 1876, and preached regularly and in various places on Sundays and holidays over the next several years. In 1882 he taught at the Islington Wesleyan Day School in Birmingham and in 1883 commenced teaching at the Jewish Collegiate School for Boys, where he first began to appreciate the influence of Jewish culture on the Scriptures. Gradually, however, doubts regarding the Scriptures' trustworthiness began to trouble his mind and heart. Morgan's struggle climaxed in a firm commitment and submission to the "Divine Library" that carried him the rest of his days. Of that decisive experience he recalled:

> For two years my Bible was shut; two years of sadness and sorrow. Strange, alluring materialistic theories were in the air, and to these I turned . . . . I became well versed in the philosophies that were the vogue in England at that time, but from them I got no relief. In my despair I took all the books that I had, placed them in a cupboard, turned the key, and there they remained

for seven years. I bought a new Bible, and began to read it with an open mind and a determined will. That Bible found me. The Book gave forth a glow, which warmed my heart, and the Word of God which I read to therein gave to my troubled soul the relief and satisfaction that I had sought for elsewhere. Since that time I have lived for one end—to preach the teaching of the Book that found me.

In May of 1888, Morgan preached a "trial sermon" before church officials, but was rejected for entrance into the Methodist ministry. His one-word telegram to his father read, "Rejected." His father's reply rang with encouragement, "Rejected on earth. Accepted in heaven. Dad." Soon after, the twenty-four year old Morgan married Annie (Nancy) and took up the pastorate at Stone Congregational Church in Staffordshire, where he was ordained in September of 1890. He pastored at Rugeley Church and Westminster Road Congregation Church, both in Birmingham, before crossing the Atlantic, the first of fifty-four times, to preach at D. L. Moody's Northfield Conference and at his Chicago Institute. From 1897 to 1901 Morgan pastored New Court Church in North London and then preached throughout the United States on behalf of the Northfield extension from 1901 to 1904, when he accepted the position of pastor at Westminster Chapel, London. Besides his pastoral duties, he continued to preach on two continents and served as president of Cheshunt College, Cambridge, England, from 1911-1914.

FOREWORD TO THE 2018 EDITION ix

Once again Morgan resigned from the pastorate, this time in 1916, in order to recover from an illness and to take up an itinerate preaching ministry, mostly in the United States and Canada. The years between 1916 and 1933 included brief pastorates in London, Cincinnati, and Philadelphia, as well as teaching positions at Biola College in Southern California and Gordon College of Theology in Boston. In his seventieth year, Morgan returned to Westminster Chapel in London, where he pastored until ill health forced him into resignation, two years before his death on May 16, 1945.

At the time of his death, he was widely known throughout Great Britain, the United States, and Canada as the "Prince of Expositors." During his lifetime G. Campbell Morgan had scrupulously avoided doctrinal and denominational controversies in order to focus on his true passion: the exposition of the Scriptures. Though too conservative for the theological liberals and too liberal for the conservatives, he was acknowledged by a broad constituency as a true man of God, wholly committed to the Revelation of God in Christ and in the Scriptures.

At Morgan's memorial service his friend and colleague, Martyn Lloyd-Jones, summed up the unique contribution of his ministry.

> The point I want to make about him as a preacher is this . . . that we are all agreed that he was God's gift to His Church. He surely was the supreme illustration of the fact that God always gives His gifts at the right time . . . . When did he come

upon the scene? It was immediately after those wonderful campaigns of D. L. Moody and Sankey in this country. There had been those great visitations of the Spirit. Men and women had been converted by the thousand. This great evangelistic movement had come into the whole life of the Church, and what was needed above everything else at that point was someone who could teach these converts. And "a man come from God" whose name was George Campbell Morgan; and he came at the critical moment, at the very right time when all those spiritual emotions and experiences needed to be harnessed and deepened and fostered. The evangelists had done their work; it was time for the teacher; and God sent him.

In fact, Campbell Morgan was a teaching preacher, focusing on the didactic, the pastoral, and the devotional aspects of the text rather than the evangelistic or theological. Morgan's major emphasis rested on explaining the meaning of the text by placing it in its concentric contexts: first, the context of the verse, then the context of the paragraph or pericope, then the context of the major section of the book in which it was found, then the context of the book, then the context of the Old or New Testament, and ultimately the context of the entire Bible. It would be fair to say that his messages were text-centered/text-focused, resembling more a lecture or lesson than a sermon, until the very end when he would surface the relevance of the message briefly, but urgently. Indeed, one reviewer has noted that, "When Morgan opened up [the text] to his congregation, they immediately saw the application to their situation and were challenged to act on that faith. Morgan is one preacher who is rarely guilty of overkill in his applications. He has a way of opening up the Scriptures and allowing his listeners to draw the consequences" (Old 880). Of course, Morgan's more biblically literate listeners and his lengthy expositions would have made the need for labored application less necessary than in twenty-first century contexts where the audiences know less and less of the Bible's message and the sermon lasts from fifteen to thirty minutes. The contemporary preacher should take Morgan's systematic method of preparation, along with his practical strategies for implementing the message of the text into a sermon and apply them to contemporary homiletical contexts that require greater emphasis on the audience and application than was necessary in Morgan's day.

What will the reader discover in *Preaching*? Just the basics of exposition, but in vintage Morgan style. Readers virtually hear the words flow from the teacher's lips as naturally and familiarly as if he had addressed the topic a hundred times. Ready examples give explicit clarity and practical access to the text's general principles. The energy of the master expositor's enthusiasm for his subject charges on nearly every page. Here is a man who believes in preaching.

The text addresses four broad themes. First, Morgan identifies truth, clarity, and passion as the essentials of any sermon. Because God's truth will be gleaned from His trustworthy revelation, the sermon will be characterized by authority. The sermon's words, structure, and delivery (diction) must be clearly understood by those who are listening. Passion results from the message moving the preacher as he preaches the truth that has already gripped, mastered, and possessed him.

Second, Morgan outlines the reason for the text, the choice of the text and the treatment of the text. The reason[s] the preacher must take a biblical text is because it gives him the authority of the Word of God, because it places specific limits on the development of his subject, and because it guards against the repetition of favorite themes. The choice of the text emerges from one's regular reading, some special need within the congregation, a definite doctrinal teaching, or from the greatness of the text itself. A proper treatment of the text demands that it be viewed in its proper contexts and, most importantly, that the message is actually in the Bible.

Third, the central message of the sermon provides an elaboration of the meaning of the text. That meaning must be proclaimed, explained, and applied. Discovering the real meaning and intention of the text demands disciplined, personal study followed by a critical exposure to commentaries and other tools. The structure or divisions of the message play a crucial role, both in presenting the development of the text clearly and in causing the listener to understand its implications and applications.

Finally, introductions must introduce, preparing the audience to attend to both the preacher and the subject, and conclusions must conclude, bringing the listeners to the point of rendering a verdict and constraining their wills toward yielding to the highest and the best.

Morgan's *Preaching* does not allege to cover the subject exhaustively. Rather, it is selectively essential. The principles expressed in this compact volume will guide yet another generation into excellence in exposition. Prepare to enter a distant time and place, yet listen for concepts that ring true through the ages.

Dr. Timothy S. Warren
Dallas, Texas

FOREWORD

IF THERE is any excuse for this book, it is that it is an attempt to answer a question that I have been asked, certainly hundreds of times during the course of my work of preaching. The question has taken many forms, but it is essentially the same. It is an enquiry concerning methods of preparation in expository preaching. Individual preachers and groups of preachers have asked me to tell them how I work. I have always felt it difficult to reply. During the three years in which I was President of Cheshunt College, Cambridge, I attempted to talk to the students on the subject. The notes of what I then said are embodied in these Lectures. In 1925 I gave them to the students of the Biblical Seminary in New York. They then appeared in condensed form in the *Biblical Review*. I have now simply taken these reprints, and recast them.

In so far as "Rules" are found here, they may be largely ignored, for, as I have said in the course of these studies, no man can make "Rules" for another. But I hold that the principles set forth are of fundamental importance and vital value in preaching.

In sending the book forth, I hope it may be

found of some help to those who, believing in the supreme place of preaching, are desirous of some guidance in the sacred work.

G. CAMPBELL MORGAN.

Westminster Chapel,
London.

EDITOR'S PREFACE TO THE 2018 REPRINT EDITION

At Long Last

SHORTLY BEFORE the 2007 release of In the Shadow of Grace: The Life and Meditations of G. Campbell Morgan, I requested and received permission from The Campbell Morgan Trust to re-issue Morgan's Preaching (1925/1937) lectures as a companion to that dark, yet delightful, biography.

I am, therefore, deeply indebted to Richard, Howard, and John (Morgan's grandsons) for allowing me, at long last, to proceed with this project. A special Note of Thanks is directed to Howard who sent me a copy of The Sermon on The Wreck of the Titanic at the beginning stages of this project. The Sermon appears as an Addendum to Preaching.

Thanks also, to Wendy Bird, formerly at Westminster Chapel, London, for providing significant back issues of The Westminster Record.

A brief line is not enough space to covey my profound gratitude to Dr's Timothy Scott Warren and Peter A. Verkruyse for their essays, which appear in this homiletical masterpiece, by G Campbell Morgan.

Additionally, a word of appreciation, is directed to Hannah Harris (Wipf & Stock) for her commitment to the completion of this project. We are, indeed, grateful!

EDITOR'S PREFACE

To Barb, Kiersten and Garrett, my wife and children – you are the center and joy of my life.

In Calvin Miller's The Sermon Maker: Tales of A Transformed Preacher God sends Sermoniel, the Angel of Homiletics, to cure Pr Sam of his "Homileticus Horribilis." Preacher Sam was "telling the truth without being owned by it." He had, therefore, lost his passion. The cure? Pr Sam was to "redefine the source of the sermon." But how? Pr Sam utilized all the latest commentaries and "homiletical tools." Yet his sermons lacked "music." Sermoniel informed Pr Sam that study and tools have their place but the true source of powerful preaching required much more. What? "... great preaching grows only from the soil of great lives." And "greatness of spirit results from our passions, our drive to care about something supremely important."

Dr Wayne Shaw, formerly Professor of Preaching and Dean of Lincoln Christian Seminary (Lincoln, Illinois), spent most of his living years teaching seminarians, and a few undergraduates, both the proper utilization of exegetical tools/homiletical devices, in addition to, pointing to the One true source and power of "great preaching." How? Dr Shaw has lived a great life consumed by a deep love of God, the Church, his students, and those who are lost without the redeeming grace of God in and through Jesus Christ. In humility and tears, this volume is dedicated to this godly and gracious Herald of God.

Dr. Kurt Iver Johanson
Advent/Winter 2017-2018

CONTENTS

*Foreword to the 2018 Edition by
Dr. Timothy S. Warren | v*

Foreword by G. Campbell Morgan | xv

Editor's Preface by Dr. Kurt I. Johanson | xvii

I. The Essentials of a Sermon | 1

II. The Text | 31

III. The Central Message | 48

IV. The Introduction and Conclusion | 72

Afterword by Dr. Peter Verkruyse | 83

Appendix | 102

I

THE ESSENTIALS OF A SERMON

IN EPHESIANS 4:8-12, verses 9 and 10 constitute a parenthesis. These verses are important, but if for the moment we leave them out, we gain a continuity of thought and statement.

"Wherefore He saith,
When He ascended on high, He led captivity captive,
And gave gifts unto men.
. . . And He gave some to be apostles" (the words 'to be' are quite unnecessary; though put in by the translators to make good sense they do not make good sense); "and some, prophets; and some, evangelists; and some, pastors and teachers; for the perfecting of the saints, unto the work of ministering, unto the building up of the body of Christ."

These gifts are not for the work of ministering, but for the perfecting of the saints, unto the work of ministering. He gave them in order that those possessing them might perfect the saints unto the work of the ministry. That work can only be fulfilled by all the saints.

In Romans 10:12-15, we read:

> "For there is no distinction between Jew and Greek: for the same Lord is Lord of all, and is rich unto all that call upon Him: for, Whosoever shall call upon the name of the Lord shall be saved. How then shall they call on Him in Whom they have not believed? and how shall they believe in Him Whom they have not heard? and how shall they hear without a preacher? and how shall they preach, except they be sent? even as it is written, How beautiful are the feet of them that bring glad tidings of good things!"

The reading of these passages introduces us to an atmosphere. Behind the subject of preaching is that of the specific Christian ministry, constituted by the gifts bestowed by the Holy Spirit upon some within the Church. The whole question of the ministry is involved in that of preaching. Men or women called into this special ministry of preaching are so called by the bestowment of a gift, whatever the gift may be. They should not be confused. I think we are making a great mistake in much of our thinking and training when we imagine that every Christian minister ought to be somewhat of an apostle, somewhat of a prophet, somewhat of an evangelist, and somewhat of a pastor and teacher. I believe that to-day in the

THE ESSENTIALS OF A SERMON 3

Christian Church these gifts are entirely distinct. But preaching is the vocation of all of them. The apostle, the prophet, the evangelist, and the pastor and teacher are called to preach. I am now concerned with preaching.

The supreme work of the Christian minister is the work of preaching. This is a day in which one of our great perils is that of doing a thousand little things to the neglect of the one thing, which is preaching.

I commend the gathering together of all the words in the New Testament—and of course I mean the Greek New Testament—that refer to the exercise of speech for the impartation of truth. We find eight or ten different Greek words, every one indicating some phase of this work of preaching. There are two however which are supreme. In our translations they are not always made distinct. All the rest are incidental, though valuable, *Euaggelizo* and *kerusso* are the words, which indicate the supreme phases of our preaching, and show us the whole New Testament ideal thereof.

Euaggelizo means to preach the Gospel. The one word is translated by our phrase, "preach the Gospel." Literally it means the proclamation of good news. It is the word from which we derive our words "evangel," "evangelist," and "evangelistic," which come directly by transliteration, rather than by translation, from the Greek word.

If preaching is proclaiming good news, that suggests two things: the need of man, and the grace of God. Those two things are postulated by the very word that is used to describe preaching from the New Testament standpoint. Proclamation of the good news to men will suggest that men are needing good news. Human need is the background. All the race's sin and sorrow and perplexity are implied. Then, of course, it recognises the whole fact of grace, that stupendous fact of Divine revelation, the grace of God. Preaching as proclaiming good news postulates human need and Divine grace. Whenever we preach, we stand between those two things, between human need and Divine grace. We are the messengers of that grace to that need.

The other word, *kerusso,* is a very interesting term, meaning really a proclamation from a throne. The word is spoken as being delivered by a messenger on behalf of a ruler. Consequently in the use of the word we have two ideas again to note: the authorising Throne, and therefore the consequent claim that the messenger is called upon to make.

Merge these two things very briefly. What is preaching? It has a hundred particulars and varieties and intonations. But here is the unifying thought. Preaching is the declaration of the grace of God to human need on the authority of the Throne of God; and it demands on the part of those who hear that they show obedience to the thing declared.

THE ESSENTIALS OF A SERMON

I once heard a man at a ministerial conference say: "In the old days preaching was a conflict between the preacher and the crowd. He was in the presence of the crowd to compel the crowd to submission. That day has gone. The preacher's vocation has changed."

I wonder! I think, if preaching has failed, or if it is failing, that is why.

The preacher should never address a crowd without remembering that his ultimate citadel is the citadel of the human will. He may travel along the line of the emotions, but he is after the will. He may approach along the line of the intellect, but he is after the will. When preaching becomes merely discussion in the realm of the intellect, or—forgive my use of the word—fooling in the realm of the emotions, and when preaching ends in the intellectual or emotional, it fails. It is successful only when it is able to storm the will, under the will of God. The preacher comes with good news; but he does not come with something to be trifled with. His message has in it an insistent demand, because he comes from a King.

That is our principal work in the Christian ministry. The apostles said; "We will continue stedfastly in prayer, and in the service (or ministry) of the Word" (Acts 6:4). That was the origin of the order of the New Testament deacons. Whatever the deacons may be now, that tells what they were then. In the New Testament they were men full of faith and the Holy Spirit. Mark the principle of appointing Church officers in the first Churches. Their business was to serve tables, a great ministry, in order that ministers of the Word might be free to serve the Word, and to give themselves to prayer in preparation.

I am deeply conscious of the baldness of human speech, but the bigness of the work, if we are to be preachers will at once recognised. Preaching is a great thing. Bishop Frazer said some few years ago—and I think it is more true to-day than it was then: "This age wants, demands, and is prepared to receive, not the priest, but the prophet."

We are facing to-day the biggest hour the world has ever known for preaching. The miseries of theological controversy that are blighting our age cannot satisfy. The mass of men are waiting for preaching of the New Testament kind, with a great message of grace to meet human need, delivered by men who realise that they represent a Throne, and have the right to claim submission to it.

I want to indicate now the essentials of a sermon, and the essentials of sermonizing. These essentials are Truth, Clarity, Passion.

I am speaking out of my experience. I never heard a lecture on homiletics in my life. I have given a good many. One fine preparation for lecturing on homiletics is never to have heard anybody else do it! I have tried to examine in the New Testament, and in the Old Testament, the

THE ESSENTIALS OF A SERMON 7

great preaching of both the prophets of the Old and the apostles and evangelists of the New. And if I am asked to condense into words the essentials of a sermon, I do it with these three: Truth, Clarity, Passion.

I use this word *Truth* now in one way. In writing to Timothy, Paul charged him in that final letter, so poignant and yet so wonderful, "Preach the Word." The verb means to proclaim as a herald, with authority. His message was to be the Word. Take the phrase, "the word," and examine its use in the New Testament. There are some places where it is spelled with a capital W, and elsewhere it is spelled without a capital W. We ask: Why is it spelled with a capital W here, and without a capital W there?

We read in John, in that matchless Prologue:

"In the beginning was the Word, and the Word was with God, and the Word was God."

And then, skipping the parenthesis:

"And the Word became flesh."

We find a capital W in every case.

Then we turn to the Gospel of Luke, and read that great Preface, so important to all the historical documents in our Bible, and he speaks of those who were "eyewitnesses and ministers of the word." Here we find a small w. Why the difference? If I am asked, Why have the translators rendered it with a small w here, instead of a capital? my answer is, I do not know. There is no reason why. We have the definite article in both places. "The word" is Luke's last name for the Son of man. Of course a preface is always written last. He wrote this preface after the Gospel was written, to introduce it to his friend Theophilus, and in it he calls Jesus "the Word."

What does this word mean? Bear with me if I condense by quoting from one of my books:

"The word Logos is used in the New Testament in two ways, the suggestiveness of each never being wholly absent from the other. Its first and perhaps simplest meaning is that of speech and language, the expression of truth for the understanding of others. Its second and perhaps deeper meaning is that of the absolute truth itself. As Thayer indicates, in that sense the Greek word Logos is the exact equivalent of the Latin word *Ratio,* from which we obtain our words *rational* and *reason.* Note the significance of that. Thus Logos is speech, and the truth spoken, or reason, and the explanation of its expression. The interrelation of ideas in their use is that the Word incarnate was the truth of God, but being the speech of God, was the expression of eternal truth. The Word and reason must express the idea in a speech which is logical and true. It is necessary, in the study of the New Testament, carefully to discriminate by reference to the context as to which sense is intended when this word is used. Some-

THE ESSENTIALS OF A SERMON 9

times it refers to speech as a statement made, sometimes to the essential truth out of which the statement came, sometimes both ideas are most evidently present in the use of the word."

It will be granted that preachers are to preach the Word. You say that means the Bible. Does it? Yes. Is that all? No. Yes, it is all there. But you want more than that, more than all. The Word is truth as expressed or revealed. The Word is never something that I have found out by the activity of my own intellectual life. The Word is something which my intellectual life apprehends, because it has been expressed. If we take the 119th Psalm and study it through—that great psalm concerning the Word of God—we are not to imagine that it is referring only to the *Torah* or Law, the *Nebiim* or Prophets, the *Kethubim* or Writings. It has in view the truth, the essential truth, and the truth as God makes it known. All that is focussed in Christ for us as preachers; and Christ is revealed to us through this literature.

But it may be asked: Isn't there an experience of Christ? There is, but the literature tests the experience. That was a tremendous description that Justin Martyr gave when, speaking of the Word of God he referred to "the spermatic Word." Seed, that is to say, the truth in germ and norm. That is what we have in the Christ, and which we find in our Bible—germ and norm.

Apply that to the Bible; what then have we? Truth in germ, which needs apprehension, development, application. That is the work of the preacher. But we also have it in norm. This means that we are to test our own thinking by it finally, and not it by our own thinking. Consequently the preacher is to be held by the Word, truth, as it is in God, and as God has made it known. How has He made it known? We are assuming without any argument that God has made it known finally in His Son, and that in the literature, the Biblical literature, we have the full record of preparation, of historic fact, of initial interpretation. Follow the line of that. Preparation, all the Old Testament. Historic fact, the four Gospel narratives. Initial interpretation, all the twenty-one letters. There we have all the literature around this one great Person, Who is in that sense for us the Word.

And that is what we have to preach. God's revelation, the truth, as it has been expressed. We must enter upon the Christian ministry on the assumption that God has expressed Himself in His Son, and that the Bible is the literature of that self-expression. The minute we lose our Bible in that regard, we have lost Christ as the final revelation. I don't want to be controversial, but you will find it is always so. Let me speak with profound respect of the men who have suffered this loss. Here is a man who for some reason refuses the authority of his Bible, but says he will stand by Christ. What Christ?

There is a fashion to-day among some preachers,

THE ESSENTIALS OF A SERMON

to talk and preach about the approach to Jesus. We are being told that we must go back and approach Him as His early disciples did. Did we ever realise the utter fallacy of that position? Those men apprehended Him in the days of His limitation, when He Himself had to say:

> "I came to cast fire upon the earth; and what do I desire, if it is already kindled? But I have a baptism to be baptized with; and how am I straitened till it be accomplished!" (Luke 12:49.50).

Ponder the significance of that—Christ's great soliloquy in this chapter in Luke in which He expressed His difficulty, that He could not make Himself known, could not fulfil His mission. He was straitened. The teaching of Christ is not the final fact about Christ, and His Person is not the final fact about Christ. We find that fact in Jesus crucified, risen, and ascended. We must approach Christ thus, and we must cling to that Christ. That is the Word of God in all its fullness.

Every sermon, then, is a message out of that sum totality of truth. Any sermon that fails to have some interpretation of that holy truth is a failure. That totality is not a small thing. In Him are summed up all things. In Him dwells the fulness, the *pleroma*, of the Godhead corporeally. The man who begins to preach Christ as the Divine revelation, interpreted to him through the literature, is beginning a thing that will never end. He can never be at the end of his message, because his message is the infinite and full and eternal truth. Preaching is the declaration of truth, as truth has been revealed to men by God, in Christ.

Take the word "mystery" as we find it in the New Testament. What do we mean by a mystery? Ordinarily it means something that we cannot understand. The Greek philosopher meant by it something that can be made known only to the initiated, and which, being made known, cannot be told to any other than those initiated. That is not the meaning of "mystery" in the New Testament. There, a mystery is something which human intellect can apprehend when it is revealed. "Great is the mystery of godliness." Paul does not mean godliness is something we cannot understand. The deep heart and meaning of godliness is beyond the discovery of the human intellect; it is something revealed. Put "manifest" over against "mystery". Being manifested, it can be apprehended.

Here is our richness, if we are going to preach. The preacher is a steward of the mysteries of God, not things that cannot be apprehended, but things that human intellect cannot discover, which God has revealed. The New Testament preacher is always moving in the realm of the supernatural. It is absurd for a man to say that he rules out the supernatural when he cuts out the little things he calls miracles—I mean little by comparison. All the miracles of Jesus, what men call miracles,

THE ESSENTIALS OF A SERMON 13

are very secondary and unimportant compared with what He said, and finally insignificant by the side of Himself and His mighty Word. The words of Jesus are far more supernatural than the things He did, if by miracle we mean some activity in the realm of the material things. We have to deal with the supernatural. All preachers must. Preachers have been told that they have been too other-worldly. When we cease to be other-worldly we lose our ability to touch this world with any healing and uplifting power. We move in the realm of truth revealed, coming to men from God.

That forces us to distinguish. Preaching is not the proclamation of a theory, or the discussion of a doubt. A man has a perfect right to proclaim a theory of any sort, or to discuss his doubts. But that is not preaching. "Give me the benefit of your convictions, if you have any. Keep your doubts to yourself; I have enough of my own," said Goethe. We are never preaching when we are hazarding speculations. Of course we do so. We are bound to speculate sometimes. I sometimes say: 'I am speculating; stop taking notes.' Speculation is not preaching. Neither is the declaration of negations preaching. Preaching is the proclamation of the Word, the truth as the truth has been revealed.

Our deposit is the sum totality of the truth. We are holding a bigger thing than we know. If we should live and preach for half a century or a century, we should never be able to exhaust the thing that is ours as a deposit. Paul wrote:

> "I know Whom I have believed, and I am persuaded that He is able to guard that which I have committed unto Him against that day."

I am not so sure that this is correct translation. It is an attempt to interpret. It is literally translated, "to guard my deposit." Our translators have always made it mean something Paul had deposited with Him. I think it means rather that which He had deposited with Paul, the thing for which he was responsible; this whole truth, this Word of God, focussed, crystalised in a Person, and interpreted by a literature.

That is our business as preachers. "Oh, but the preacher must catch the spirit of the age." God forgive him if he does. Our business is never to catch, but by eternal truth to correct the spirit of the age. This is not narrow. Nothing can happen to-day to which the truth of God has not something to say. Our preaching will touch life at every point. We do not go to discuss a situation, but to deliver a message. The preacher must for evermore stand in the presence of man and conditions, thinking in his own soul, if the formula is not often upon his lips, "Thus saith the Lord." Here is the truth, the truth that men never have been able to discover by all the exercise, honest and sincere and persistent, of their intellectual activity, but the truth that God has spoken, revealed, made known.

(See Hebrews I:1-4) He has spoken to us in a Son. The great fact is God, God speaking, making Himself known in the past in divers portions and by divers manners, at last in a Person, Who gathered up the portions and uttered them in one inclusive final revelation. When we enter the Christian ministry and become preachers, it is that whole body of truth for which we are responsible.

By truth I mean the Word, in all the fulness of the suggestiveness of that expression. May I say again that by that I mean the revelation, God's Self-revelation of Himself, centrally, supremely, finally in His Son. But, of course, also in the literature that is in the Bible. Preaching is declaring the truth of God as it bears upon every local situation. "Preach the Word."

As I said, every sermon is an interpretation, or should be an interpretation, of some part of that great whole of truth. Every sermon is characterised by two things—originality and authority.

I am going to make a long quotation. Some thirty-five or more years ago I wrote this out for myself, and I have kept it by me, and very often have read it. It is on *originality*. Men were constantly using that term "original", insisting that the preacher must be original. We have heard it said in criticism of a sermon, "It was very good, but it was not original." We should realise what originality really is, therefore I give this somewhat lengthy quotation from Shedd:

"Originality is a term often employed, rarely defined, and very often misunderstood. It is frequently supposed to be equivalent to the creation of truth. An original mind, it is vulgarly imagined, is one that gives expression to ideas and truths that were never heard of before,—ideas and truths 'of which the human mind never had even an intimation or presentiment, and which come into it by a mortal leap, abrupt and startling, without antecedents and without premonitions.' But no such originality as this is possible to a finite intelligence. Such aboriginality as this is the prerogative of the Creator alone, and the results of it are a *revelation,* in the technical and strict sense of the term. Only God can create *de nihilo,* and only God can make a communication of truth that is absolutely new. Originality in man is always relative, and never absolute. Select, for illustration, an original thinker within the province of philosophy,—select the contemplative, the profound, the ever fresh and living Plato. Thoughtfully peruse his weighty and his musical periods, and ask yourself whether all this wisdom is the sheer make of his intellectual energy, or whether it is not rather an emanation and efflux from a mental *constitution* which is as much yours as his. He did not absolutely originate these first truths of ethics, these necessary forms of logic, these fixed principles of physics. They were inlaid in his rational structure by a higher author, and by an absolute authorship; and his originality consists

THE ESSENTIALS OF A SERMON 17

solely in their exegesis and interpretation. And this is the reason that, on listening to his words, we do not seem to be hearing tones that are wholly unknown and wholly unheard of. We find an answering voice to them in our mental and moral constitution. In no contemptuous, but in a reverential and firm tone, every thinking person, even in the presence of the great thinkers of the race, may employ the language of Job, in reference to self-evident truths and propositions:

> 'Lo, mine eye hath seen all this, mine ear hath heard and understood it.
> What ye know, the same do I know also; I am not inferior unto you.' "

This quotation from Job is wonderfully apt at this point. Every one who listens to us when we are giving him something original is saying that thing.

"And these great thinkers themselves are the first to acknowledge this . . . Originality then, within the sphere of a creature, and in reference to a finite intelligence, consists in the power of interpretation. In its last analysis it is *exegesis,*—the pure, genial, and accurate exposition of an idea or a truth already existing, already communicated, already possessed. . . . There has been no creation, but only a development; no absolute authorship, but only an explication. And yet how fresh and original has been the mental process! The same substantially in Plato and in the thousands of his scholars; and yet in every single instance there has been all the enthusiasm, all the stimulation, all the ebullient flow of life and feeling that attends the discovery of a new continent or a new star.

> 'Then feels he like some watcher of the skies
>   When a new planet swims into his ken;
> Or like stout Cortez, when with eagle eyes
>   He stared at the Pacific, and all his men
> Looked at each other with a wild surmise,
>   Silent, upon a peak in Darien.'

"Originality in man, then, is not the power of making a communication of truth, but of apprehending one. Two great communications have been made to him,—the one in the book of nature, and the other in the book of revelation. If the truth has been conveyed through the mental and moral structure, if it has been wrought by the creative hand into the fabric of human nature, then he is the most original thinker who is most successful in reading it just as it reads, and expounding it just as it stands. If the truth has been communicated by miracle, by incarnation, and by the Holy Ghost; if it has been imparted by special inspiration, and lies before him an objective and written revelation; then he is the original thinker who is most successful in its interpretation,—who is most accurate in analysing its living elements, and is most genial and cordial in re-

THE ESSENTIALS OF A SERMON 19

ceiving them into his own mental and moral being."*

This quotation is one of the statements that have profoundly influenced my life, my working, and my preaching. We see where that takes the question of originality. If indeed, our deposit as preachers is that sum total of truth, contained in the Word, which we face in order to interpret, in the written Word, we shall always be original. Not that we are inventing new truths, or even discovering them, but that we are interpreting the sum total of truth by every Christian sermon that has in it the originality of the apprehension of the meaning of revealed truth, and of giving it to others that they may apprehend it. That originality is a note of real preaching. A man who is merely indulging in speculation, along the ways of his own thinking, is never original. Originality in preaching consists in the interpretation of revelation. Revelation is so great and mighty, that if we are dealing with that, and always leading into it, in every message, there is always something original in our preaching.

A sermon should be characterised also by *authority*. In the seventh chapter of Matthew there is a little paragraph which Matthew wrote with reference to the effect produced upon the multitude by what we call the Sermon on the Mount—rather

* *Homiletics and Pastoral Theology*, William G. T. Shedd. P. 7ff.

the great ethical manifesto of the King—concerning the effect upon the multitude:

> "And it came to pass, when Jesus had finished these words, the multitudes were astonished at His teaching; for He taught them as One having authority, and not as their scribes" (Matt 7:28,29).

Has it ever occurred to us that the remarkable thing is not the declaration that He spake as One having authority, though that is the main thing? What arrests us?

> "The multitudes were astonished at His teaching; for He taught them as One having authority, and *not as their scribes.*"

The arresting thing in that statement is the little phrase which makes that distinction or contrast. I could read it over and over again, and agree. Of course, when He spake He had authority. But the thing that arrested me long ago, and still holds me is the contrast suggested, "not as their scribes."

The scribes were the authoritative teachers. An order of scribes was not arranged for in the Mosaic economy. They came with Ezra. When Ezra erected that pulpit of wood, and held what we can probably call the first Bible conference on record, he "read the law, and gave the sense." This means first that he was translating it from Hebrew into the language of the Captivity; but it

THE ESSENTIALS OF A SERMON

means more. He interpreted and applied it. So arose the order of scribes. Their work was that of moral interpretation. They were the authoritative teachers, whom our Lord recognised. In Matthew 23 He said:

> "The scribes and the Pharisees sit on Moses' seat; all things therefore whatsoever they bid you, these do and observe"—

but don't do as they do. That is a startling thing. While not appointed in the Mosaic economy at the beginning, their authority was recognised, and our Lord also acknowledged it. They surely spoke with authority. And yet Matthew says: "He spoke as One having authority, but not as their scribes."

The authority detected in the teaching of Jesus was not of the nature of the authority detected in the teachings of the scribes. What was the difference? The authority of the scribes consisted in their recognised position, in the fact that they were chosen to be the interpreters of the Law of Moses. It was the authority of the office conferred and exercised. What was the difference? He spoke as One having authority, but not that way. I do not think this authority was to be found in His demeanour, in His attitude, in His look, though I don't think, if we had seen our Lord in the days of His flesh and listened to Him, we would have missed the dignity and wonder of His personality. His authority was rather the authority of the thing

He said, as it found them and found in them an answer of acquiescence.

Take the Sermon on the Mount. I am referring to it generally, of course. Is it not arresting, at least that we do not find men quarrelling with that to-day? I mean those that we differ from, who to our thinking emasculate the Person of Christ and deny what we call the supernatural, the miraculous, still hold the Sermon on the Mount, because they cannot quarrel with it. Human consciousness never quarrels with it.

There is only one criticism of the ethical ideals of the Sermon on the Mount that is justified, at least so far as I know. What is it? Take that Sermon on the Mount and read it through. Study it. See what it has to say about individual life, about social relationships, knowing the great passion of the ultimate glory of the Kingdom of God that flames and flashes through its ideals. Where do men quarrel with it, not as Christians, but as human beings? At what point can they object? There is only one justifiable criticism, and that does not deny its beauty or its glory. It is that it is not practicable. I mean that no unregenerate man can live by the Sermon on the Mount. I am told to preach it to the world. I decline to do it, because men cannot obey it. It must be held up as a revelation of God's ideal, but no man can obey it unless he is born again.

Remember that our Lord did not give the Sermon on the Mount to the outside world. He gave

THE ESSENTIALS OF A SERMON 23

it to His disciples. The outside world heard it. They gathered about. But He was giving the Law of the Kingdom to those who were submitted to the King. The multitudes merely gathered and listened. We are to insist upon that standard of life, but to do that apart from the preaching of the Evangel, which brings something dynamic, is merely to reveal man's impotence. You cannot run human life on the basis of the Sermon on the Mount, until people are born again. It is too high, too severe.

The sermon which is a true interpretation of any part of that sum totality of truth which we have in the Word is original, because it is a true interpretation of that which is the revelation, and to us carries the conviction of truth, which is authority. That is where the authority of the preacher lies; not in a demeanour, not even in formulated creeds that are behind him, though I do not speak disrespectfully of them, but in the thing he says. If his sermon is an exposition, interpretation, and application of some part of truth, it always carries authority.

It is very remarkable that the Old Testament prophets made their occasional appeal, not merely to the people to whom they talk, but to a wider world, for confirmation. In Jeremiah we find a point where he used a common word in a most remarkable way. He said, "You have refused your God, therefore your God will refuse you." And again, "Men will call you refuse silver, because Jehovah hath refused you" (Jer 6:30). It was a play on words. Jeremiah told those people that men outside the nation would agree with God's action in the nation. They would account the people refuse, who had refused God, and who were refused of God. He was appealing to an underlying human consciousness.

The preacher always has that to appeal to. I am not going to be involved in an argument concerning original sin. I believe in it; I have seen so much of it in others, and found so much more of it in myself. But God has never left Himself without witness. The libertine—any man—who listens to your sermon, if it is a Biblical denunciation of sin, the outflashing of what the Word of God has to say about sin, recognises the truth. It has authority. We come away from the Word to the disputes of men, and they will not believe us, even though Sir Oliver Lodge is the preacher. He told us no intelligent man worries about sin or disputes about sin. A more unscientific thing was never said by a scientist. Not that men call it sin; they call it continuous abnormality, and all sorts of things, but they know the fact. The message of the Word on the subject always reaches that underlying consciousness. I am not saying that they will obey. That is not our business. We are to preach the truth with that exegesis which means a true exposition of the truth itself, and that always has the note of authority.

Again every sermon should have *clarity*. Of

THE ESSENTIALS OF A SERMON

course I mean clarity of statement in every way. Martin Luther said: "A preacher ought so to preach, that when the sermon is ended, the congregation shall disperse saying, 'The preacher said this.'"

The whole point, as I understand it is, that the sermon should have a message that is perfectly clear in its statement of something that grips the congregation, so that they would go away saying, "The preacher said this." Clarity. In preaching everything should be subservient to this.

Here another thing to be remembered is, that the making plain does not depend upon us finally, but upon the Holy Spirit. The preaching of the Word must be in the demonstration and power of the Holy Spirit, not power only, but demonstration, the making plain. When the Christian preacher, preaching out of His Word, is true to His will, he may know that in co-operation with him—I use the word reverently, but reasonably—is the Holy Spirit making the Word plain. But no man has any right to depend wholly upon that. In the preparation and delivery of a sermon we must be very careful that we make our statement such as can be apprehended by those who are listening. That applies to diction, illustrations, and manner of delivery. We preach in order that people may apprehend.

Our diction comes under that heading. It is told of Robert Hall, that great English preacher of a couple of generations ago—than whom we never had in some senses, a greater preacher, a man who preached for forty years, never out of physical pain—that he had a manuscript of his own sent in for correction, and he stumbled over the word "felicity." He said: "Was I fool enough to use that word? Strike it out, and put in 'happiness.'"

If twenty people in the congregation don't know what it means, is it not better to strike it out, and put in 'happiness'?

I remember when a little book of mine called *Life Problems* was published, many years ago, it was very severely reviewed by a great journal. The reviewer said: "This man evidently has no use for language other than that of making people know what he wants to say." He went on to say that there were no flowers of speech, no beauties of expression. I pasted it in a book, and I said, "The Lord help me to keep right there." I urge that as something of importance in all preaching.

Clarity affects the whole question of illustrations. That is another big side issue, but I would give to every young preacher a simple formula for his illustrations. Let your illustrations be such as shine into your sermon, and not illustrations that you drag in. You have heard men preach, and tell a story. The story has really no vital relationship with their message. They put it in, and it relieves the congregation, making them smile at the moment perhaps, but it has no relation to the sermon. One of the most skilful

THE ESSENTIALS OF A SERMON   27

in this matter that I have known was John Henry Jowett. W. L. Watkinson was another. Dr. Jowett's illustrations always shone into his main theme. You never went away with the illustration as the supreme thing; it was there illuminating. I remember hearing him in Birmingham, when he said; "Human and Divine divisions of humanity are radically different. Divine divisions are perpendicular, human divisions are horizontal."

Well, there we were. He picked up his hymn book, held it upright, and said; "I will show you what I mean. That is perpendicular division to the right, to the left; that is Divine."

Then holding it flat; "This is horizontal-upper, middle, lower classes; that is human."

That is great illustration.

With the portion of truth that is constituting the sermon, with the great originality that is always in an inescapable truth, winged with its own authority, our business is in some way to make that truth have clarity in our diction, in our illustration, and of course in our manner.

Finally there is a third essential, *Passion.* I want to say a word about this quite briefly. In the true sermon there must always be passion. But the passion must be something that is created by no conscious effort. It must come out of what we are declaring, and out of our consciousness of it. Half the sermons to-day—may I be forgiven if I am cruel—are failing because they lack the note of passion. There is a tale told of that great English actor Macready. An eminent preacher once said to him:

"I wish you would explain something to me."

"Well, what is it? I don't know that I can explain anything to a preacher."

"What is the reason for the difference between you and me? You are appearing before crowds night after night with fiction, and the crowds come wherever you go. I am preaching the essential and unchangeable truth, and I am not getting any crowd at all."

Macready's answer was this: "This is quite simple. I can tell you the difference between us. I present my fiction as though it were truth; you present your truth as though it were fiction."

I leave that story right at this point. Of course the question comes, whether a man can preach these things without passion if they are truth to him. I don't know; I must not sit in judgment on other men. But our theme as preachers of the Word has to do with the glory of life—with the tragedy of sin, and its remedy. I cannot see how any one can really handle these things until he is handled by them. A man was formerly said to "handle his text." If he handles his text he cannot preach at all. But when his text handles him, when it grips and masters and possesses him, and in experience he is responsive to the thing he is declaring, having conviction of the supremacy of truth and experience of the power of truth, I think that must create passion.

I am not arguing for mere excitement. Painted fire never burns, and an imitated enthusiasm is the most empty thing that can possibly exist in a preacher. Given the preacher with a message from the whole Bible, seeing its bearing on life at any point, I cannot personally understand that man not being swept sometimes right out of himself by the fire and the force and the fervour of his work.

Truth, clarity, passion—I believe that in the real sermon these three things are always found.

Truth will always, in my view, make its impression of authority upon the soul, but we cannot get it over to the soul save as it comes through our own personality, not merely as an intellectual concept, but as a thing that is moving us. I don't think any preacher ever can lift his hearers above the level of his own experience. That is a great conviction with me. We cannot take our people, even if we state truth accurately, if it is only an intellectual statement, and make them feel its force. That is the difference between the press and the pulpit. Read a book, and we have the truth perhaps, but in preaching you have the truth plus the man, not plus as though we can separate them, but the truth incarnate expressing itself to me through man.

Truth and life travel together in preaching. He

Who said, "I am the truth," also said, "I am the life." In Him we have the eternal illustration of the power of truth in life. In a measure that has to be reproduced in all who are really preaching. Of course, it is a very different thing from lecturing, or discussing things with the congregation. That does not concern us. Our business is uttering the Word of God.

II

THE TEXT

BY "TEXT" we mean the paragraph, the verse, or part of a verse, which is the basis of a sermon. Preaching from texts has become an established custom in the Christian Church in all denominations. Whether in the Greek Church or the Roman Church, or the Churches of Protestantism, preachers take texts. It seems to be one of those decisions of the universal Church, which demonstrate the guidance of the Spirit of God far more than any formulas or decrees ever have done or can do. This method has come out of the common feeling and consciousness of the Christian Church and the men who have ministered in it.

The word itself, from the Latin *textum*, means something that is woven. We find it in the word texture, referring to a garment. Quoting from Dr. Shedd; "A text is a passage of inspiration, which is woven primarily into the web of Holy Writ, and secondarily, into the web of a discourse."

I like that definition. A text is primarily woven into the web of Holy Writ. That is where we find it. It is taken from there, and then it is woven into the web of the sermon. So the question of the text is of supreme importance when we are talking about sermonising.

Let us briefly take up three lines: first, the Reason for the text; second, the Choice of the text; third, the Treatment of the text.

Now as to *the Reason for the text*. Dr. Benjamin Jowett of Oxford, the old Master of Balliol, declared that it was his habit to write his sermons, and then choose a text as a peg on which to hang them. I am quite free to say, without any further reference, that the study of his sermons will reveal the accuracy of his statement, and show the peril of the method, from the standpoint of the Christian prophet.

Why have a text? Three reasons: first, the authority that is in the text as being a part of the Word of God; second, the definiteness which it must give, when properly dealt with, to the Christian message; and finally, the maintenance of variety.

First, the authority of the Word of God. The Christian preacher is a messenger. His sermon must be a message. Let us always remember that to proclaim our personal convictions may not be to deliver a message from God, and therefore, in the last analysis, is not preaching at all, except as our convictions are based upon the Word of God. There may be excellent work done in lecturing and speaking, which yet falls short of preaching. Such proclamation may not be the delivery of a message from God. I know men who are convinced of the absolute Deity of our Lord, without any qualification, but they do not believe He was born of a Virgin. If they proclaim that from the pulpit, that is the proclamation of their conviction, but that is not preaching the Word. Preaching the Word must be preaching that He was born of a Virgin. You may debate that question philosophically and scientifically, but that is not preaching. No man can be preaching the Word, unless he is delivering the Divine message. I am assuming the authority of the Bible. Preaching is nothing else than bringing God's message, as it is found in the Oracles Divine. When the sermon has a text which is authoritative, all the rest is to be tested by it.

That is the value of the text. I read a text to my congregation. That is the message. That is the one thing that is absolutely and finally authoritative. My sermon has no authority in it at all, except as an interpretation or an exposition or an illustration of the truth which is in the text. The text is everything. That is the point of authority.

Then it is not only the fact of having a point of authority; it is also so, that a text gives definiteness to the message. Limitation creates power. The fact that we are only taking that paragraph, verse, statement, perhaps phrase, gives this limitation. In preaching there is a tendency to generalisation and discursiveness. That is checked when a sermon is really true to its text.

You have authority, because the text is the Word of God. You have definiteness because you are bound to keep within the confines of what that text is saying. The text, of course, may say much in its implications and applications; but it defines the theme.

There was a man who gave out his text and said: "That is my text. I am now going to preach. Maybe we'll meet again, the text and I, and maybe not."

He was not going to preach at all; he was just going to talk.

Preaching from texts also maintains variety. Themes will run out sooner or later, but the Bible never. It affords expositions and illustrations and enforcements, and the procession of a real Biblical ministry is always maintained. If we think of any minister who has maintained his virility and his freshness through long years, especially at one centre, I think I am right in saying that his ministry has been Biblical. The freshness of the Bible is eternal.

What then, about *the Choice of the text?* How are we to choose? In many ways this is the most important part of our discussion. Every preacher comes up against that. Twice next Sunday, twice next Sunday, twice next Sunday—how many of us have gone through that? The question of the choice of texts is a critical one, and attention should be given to it at once and continuously.

THE TEXT

How is a man to choose texts? Texts are sometimes chosen out of our regular reading, sometimes in order to deal with some special need, sometimes in order to definite doctrinal teaching, and sometimes because of their revelation of great things.

Out of regular reading. From my own experience I may say that in the regular reading of the Bible devotionally, there will constantly be discovered some one text, some one statement, some one verse, which grips. When such is the case let us never hurry on. It is good to stop and put it down. Postpone further reading, until we have at least said to ourself, Why did that arrest me; what is there in that which pulled me up? Make a note of it. If we form the habit of constantly doing that in our devotional reading we shall find these things that thus seemed to leap out at us. "When found, make a note of"—Captain Cuttle's advice is very excellent. If possible we should make an outline of the scheme of thought suggested. Sometimes when we want a text, we shall run over these outlines, and perhaps not see a thing in ninety-nine per cent of them. In one per cent we shall, and that one per cent is worthwhile.

Sometimes a text will bring a ready-made sermon. That is not often the case, but it is so now and then. It is not merely a message, but a whole scheme. This happened to me once many years ago. It was during my earlier ministry in London. I had my sermon prepared for Sunday morning.

Before starting for the service I was reading in my study Peter's first letter. Often before preaching I read through some book in the Bible that has nothing to do with what I am preaching on. I struck against the ninth verse of the second chapter:

> "Ye are an elect race, a royal priesthood, a holy nation, a people for God's own possession, that ye may show forth the excellencies (praises) of Him Who called you out of darkness into His marvellous light."

The whole thing leaped at me. I looked at it, and looked at it, and then got up, went to the Church, went through the first part of the service, read the text, and preached for an hour. I know that is dangerous, yet I have preached that sermon many times since, and at present I am preparing a book on the same.

What did I see in it? Principle; "Ye are . . . that ye may." That is what gripped me. "Ye are" these things, whatever ye are, "that ye may." Then Purpose: "Ye are . . . that ye may show forth the excellencies of Him Who called you out of darkness into His marvellous light." The thing that struck me with force was the bed-rock principle of the Church—"Ye are . . . that ye may." The Church exists for a purpose. She is not self-contained. She is a means to an end. If that is true, what is the purpose? "That ye may show forth the excellencies of Him Who called you out of darkness into His marvellous light." That is the purpose, that the Church may exhibit God to the world—may show forth the excellencies of Him Who called her.

The next question that arises: How can the Church do that is answered. "Ye are"—what? "An elect race, a royal priesthood, a holy nation, a people for God's own possession." That is what she is. And in that description we are face to face with her power. In what she is lies her power. She is an elect race. The life principle is there. Priesthood—right of access to God on the basis of a life principle. Nation—true social principles within the Church for a new revelation of God to the world. Possession—no longer demon-possessed, but God-possessed. As a demon masters, obsesses, possesses, reveals himself in a man, so God masters, obsesses, possesses, reveals Himself in those who are a people for His own possession.

I never made that sermon. It came to me. I would not say that that has often occurred in my life, but sometimes it does.

Let us not run away from such an experience. Let us dare to deliver the message while it is living and virile in our minds. Plunge in at once and do it. We will never drown; we may go down several times, but we shall come up.

Let me add another thing. If we read our lessons in public, as they ought to be read, over and over again something we are reading will grip us. When we get home let us immediately make a note of it. I think I have found more fresh texts in this way than in any other. In private reading one reads perhaps a little quickly. In public reading, when endeavouring to give the emphasis and tone and interpretation without talking about it, so that the people can get it, scores of texts have come to me.

May I insert a word here with respect to the public reading of the Scripture? I don't know anything that is worse done in the Christian Church to-day than the reading of the Bible by preachers. That sounds very harsh, but I feel that it is so. There is a monotonous reading, and an academic reading, and sometimes a theatrical reading which is just as objectionable as the rest. If we could only get men to lay themselves out to read the Scripture with interpretation, quite apart from talking about it! I never read a lesson in the pulpit now without first carefully reading it at home. I may have read it scores of times, but I never go to the pulpit without reading my lesson again, and watching for its meaning. I don't mind a man stopping in the middle of his reading, to say something that will illuminate the passage, but one should do as little of it as he can. He ought to read it so that in the reading its sense is carried to the listening crowd. In the doing of it, great passages will strike us. Note them. Then we have something to turn to.

There is another method of choosing texts, which is inevitable. In the course of our ministry, especially our pastoral and prophetic work, which is distinctive, quite a little from the more directly evangelistic, we shall sometimes have to preach on some particular subject—some bereavement, some perplexity, some special need, something in our Church life, something in front of our people who are listening to us, something existing in the city that we ought to speak about. There may be some invasion of the moral realm iniquitously by the civic authorities in the city. Should we preach that sort of sermon? Most assuredly. I believe that is our business. We are to know these things and to bring the Word of God to bear upon them. That is to say, special needs must sometimes be dealt with by the preacher. For we are not merely to preach truth theoretically; we have to show the bearing of the truth upon the practical things of life. Consequently texts have to be chosen.

Dr. Dale it was who said: "The Bible is not merely a book of texts, it is a textbook. It contains the truths of the text, the ones we have to illustrate, in their relation to the lives of our people; the Divine premises by which we are to console them in trouble and to strengthen their faith in the love and power of God."

We want to remind people of that. We have never yet come to, and we never shall come to any occasion demanding a special message, but that we shall find in our Bible exactly what is needed to touch that particular condition.

When occasion arises, we must choose. Our looking will demand an acquaintance with the Bible in many ways. The Bible has something to say to every phase and every mood of human life. But to know what it has to say that is apposite, and where it has the text, demands of course a personal acquaintance that involves first-hand study. God help the man who, when some occasion demands this, has got to go to his concordance to find a text. You will hardly find it there. You may get a word that you think covers the ground, and looking it up, find that you are very far off.

Then there must be doctrinal preaching. Dr. Dale was told that people would not stand doctrinal sermons, and he replied, "They'll have to stand them," and they did stand them for forty years. There is an enormous need for the preaching of the great doctrines of the Christian Church. I do not believe that any minister is strong if he neglects them. But we have to find the doctrine in the Word. There must be the choice of those texts in which great doctrines are most simply stated. The revelation must be allowed to limit the proclamation, always.

Again, there are great themes. Let no man be afraid to attempt these because he is not able to reach finality. Dr. Alexander Maclaren once said:

"A man should begin early to grapple with great subjects, therefore he should seek for great texts. As the athlete gains might by great exertions, so a man does not overstrain his powers by taking great texts. The more he wrestles, the more he will gain strength. He must not merely dream over the subject or play with it. No two men will treat the same subject alike, unless they imitate each other. The things that agitate the world, the things that agitate your own bosoms—preach on them. The things we would like to have settled before we die—settle them and preach on them. The things you would ask an apostle if you had a chance to talk to him—get your Bible and preach on them."

Let there be daring. Take up great themes. We may have to amend a good deal of our thinking as the years go on, but don't let us be afraid to choose great texts.

Let us look briefly at some principles of choice. First of all, we take up a text because in it there is a theme. We may recall Rousseau's recipe for a love letter: "To write a good love letter you will begin without knowing what you are going to say, and end without knowing what you have said."

A sermon is exactly the reverse. We begin by knowing generally what we are going to say, and we end knowing what we have said. Hence the text must have a theme either in its actual statement or by suggestion. Let it be of compassable magnitude. I think some texts in the Bible are too small; I think some are too perfect. There is a text that I have never attempted to preach on, though I have gone around and around it—John

3:16. It is too big. When I have read it, there is nothing else to say. If we only knew how to read it, so as to produce a sense of it in the ears of people, there would be nothing to preach about.

Another good principle in choosing texts is to preach on the part of the Word of God that has rebuked us. The thing that got me, the thing that hurt me, the thing that shamed me, the thing that bowed me in penitence—I should preach. We can put experience into it. The thing that comforts me, that inspires me—I should preach on that. I don't think preaching is ever so powerful as when it comes out of the life in that sense. Not merely that the life morally conforms to the general ethic of the Bible, but that we are giving our people something that has gripped us.

I had the privilege of a great friendship with Dr. Parker in the last ripe years of his life, and I was in his vestry one day when a man came in. Dr. Parker had preached that morning a great sermon, and this man said, "I want to thank you for that sermon. It did me good." Dr. Parker looked at him, and said: "Sir, I preached it because it had done me good." He had given a message that had come out of his own life, something that had gripped him.

The preacher must see that the text is a complete statement. Watch that. For instance, we cannot preach on the text: "Work out your own salvation with fear and trembling" (Phil. 2:12). We have no right to preach on that, though I have heard men try to do so. The Bible does not say that, even though we say we can find it. Yes, we can—but we can't. We have no right to preach on the working out of our own salvation with fear and trembling, and to stop there. The next word is a conjunction: "for it is God Who worketh in you both to will and to work, for His good pleasure." We want all of it; half of it is not true. A man cannot work out his own salvation. Let the text be a complete statement.

How far are we warranted in taking phrases? We may be warranted, if we observe care. Here is a phrase, "But God." I think you would be warranted in using that. Said the rich fool:

> "And I will say to my soul, Soul, thou hast much goods laid up for many years; take thine ease, eat, drink, be merry. But God—" (Luke 12:19-20).

We cannot preach that without the context, but it is a good text. God breaking in upon the life when the light has been excluded. I think that is fair and permissible.

I once heard Dr. W. L. Watkinson preach from these words: "Thou mayest add thereto." Where do you find these words? David is dying. He is telling Solomon to build the temple. He tells Solomon all he has amassed, all he has gathered to build the temple, and that he is devoting also his own wealth to it. He says in substance: "There it is Solomon; there is all that ready for you, and 'thou mayest add thereto.'" (I Chron. 22:14). Now here is Dr. Watkinson's treatment of that. First, The limitation of every worker for God. David comes to the end, and nothing is finished. He has to say to someone else: "I have gone so far, but it is not finished; 'thou mayest add thereto.'" Every man goes out, never having finished. Second, No worker for God need sit down and chant a dirge. God always has some one to whom He can hand his work on.

I think that is fair. I have never forgotten the two great things in taking the illustration from the historical background; David had to lay down this work unfinished. Every one of us has to do the same thing; but God is there, and there is the next man coming on. "Thou mayest add thereto." That choice of a text is perfectly justified.

Another method of taking a text is that of getting a concatenation of passages, because of some relationship. Mr. Spurgeon preached one of his mightiest sermons on these words, "I have sinned." How did he treat it? He simply went through his Bible and showed that these words were used by the hardened sinner Pharaoh, by the doubleminded Balaam, by Achan with more remorse than repentence, by the insincere King Saul, by Job overwhelmed by the righteousness of God, by the prodigal son in his confession of unworthiness to the father, and by Judas in the agony of despair. That seems to be a justifiable method of choosing.

THE TEXT 45

The Treatment of the text is a subject by itself, but some suggestions on this point may be appropriate here. First of all, be sure your text is in the Bible. I heard a man preach from the words, "Abstain from all appearance of evil." Now that is in I. Thessalonians 5:22. His whole sermon was to prove that we have no right to do anything which appears to be evil, even though it is not evil. Paul never wrote such a thing as that. The word "appearance" in the King James Version simply means the appearance of a thing that is there, not a false appearance. Your Revised Version pulls you up sharply—"Abstain from every form of evil." That is a very different thing. But many Christian people understand that injunction to mean that we must not do anything that looks evil, even though it is not evil. That is misinterpretation. "Abstain from every form of evil."

I heard a sermon on The Necessity for Prayer and Fasting, based on this passage: "This kind can come forth by nothing, but by prayer and fasting" (Mark 9:29.A.V.). Scholarship has been driven to the conclusion that those words, "and fasting" were added later. Our Lord did not use them. "This kind can come out by nothing, save by prayer." (R.V.) We have not lost anything.

We know when we begin what our text is. Then the context must be considered. "Who shall dwell with the everlasting burnings?" I heard a sermon on that, on hell. Hell is not all that is there.

> "The sinners in Zion are afraid; trembling hath seized the godless ones: Who among us can dwell with the devouring fire? Who among us can dwell with everlasting burnings?"

That is the question. The answer comes in the context, immediately following:

> "He that walketh righteously and speaketh uprightly; he that despiseth the gain of oppressions, that shaketh his hands from taking a bribe, that stoppeth his ears from hearing of blood, and shutteth his eyes from looking upon evil; he shall dwell on high; his place of defence shall be the munitions of rocks; his bread shall be given him; his waters shall be sure. Thine eyes shall see the King in His beauty; they shall behold a land that reacheth afar" (Isaiah 33:14-17).

That is not hell. That is God.

The whole point is that the prophet was looking out upon Zion, and saw the sinners in Zion afraid. They had suddenly seen all the city and its surroundings held in the grasp and presence of God. God was there in the burning and the devouring fire. Who can dwell therein? Only the upright in heart. Then we get that one little passage describing their position, set on high; their defence, "the munitions of rocks"; their sustenance, bread and water sure; their hope, they shall "see the King in His beauty," and a land of magnificent distances. And all that comes when we live in fire. Thus the context is always important.

III

THE CENTRAL MESSAGE

BEING sure that our text is in the Bible, we proceed to find out its actual meaning, and then to elaborate its message. Elaboration is not destruction. Nevertheless, in the process of elaboration it is always possible, very possible and very easy, to deviate at some point from the true line of thinking, and then to continue in the deflection until one finds oneself far from the thought of the text, and sometimes even contradicting its teaching.

Elaboration is far more than simple statement. The text has postulates, implicates, deductions, applications. They are important, though not patent in a simple statement. Elaboration consists in the discovery of these things and their setting forth in such form as to make the simple statement more luminous. The sermon is the text repeated more fully, in that these things—postulates, implicates, deductions, applications—are discovered and declared, or at least recognised. Elaboration is in order to clarity. It must proceed in a systematic way in order to a systematic statement.

THE CENTRAL MESSAGE

Every sermon, then, must have a scheme, a plan, at least in the mind of the preacher, and I think that this plan should be made clear to a congregation. A great many addresses called sermons are really essays. The etymology of the two words will help us. An essay means a weighing or a trial. *The Century Dictionary* gives this definition: "In literature a discursive composition concerned with a particular subject, usually shorter and less methodical than a treatise." That is an essay. A sermon, on the other hand, is a finished and complete discourse on a given subject. Therefore the preacher should define his purpose, ere he commences his elaboration. Granted a text, a general idea is suggested. A text grows on him, and he wants to preach on it. Why? Because it says something. It says something to him. There is an idea, a general idea, created in his mind by it, or he would not take the text. To communicate that idea is his purpose. That purpose should first be defined; secondly, kept in mind through all the process of preparation; and thirdly, stated at the outset in delivery.

It is quite possible that, in the course of preparation, he will have to change his purpose, or else his text. The text fastens itself upon him. There is something in it, something that appeals to him. There is a message in it of some sort. There is something in this paragraph, verse, sentence, phrase —a definite idea. There is the purpose, the message. He wants to deliver that message. Let him write it out briefly; then start to work on the text. Again and again he will find that the thing he thought was there is not there at all. He may get another sermon out of the text, or he may go to another text to find his sermon. First, then, purpose should be defined.

Let us take a little aside at this point, as this will throw light on the whole subject of sermonising. Sermons are different in reference to method—topical, textual, or expository. They are also different in character. A sermon may be doctrinal, or it may be ethical, or it may be devotional, or it may be, to make a word cover a large ground, providential.

It may be doctrinal, not directly ethical, not necessarily apologetic, not invariably polemical. There are some men who never seem able to preach a doctrinal sermon without getting into apologetics or polemics. They are always fighting for the thing they are preaching, which is in my judgment, a questionable thing to do. But a doctrinal sermon is always didactic; it is always of teaching value. It is always in some sense philosophical. It is always practical. That ought to be recognised. It is possible to preach doctrinal sermons without saying anything of their bearing on life. But that is a great mistake. If we take any one of Paul's letters and divide it at some point into two parts, we shall find a statement of doctrine, followed by the application of doctrine to duty. There are two

THE CENTRAL MESSAGE 51

sorts of preachers who seem to fail in this regard. There are those who pay no attention to the doctrines of our faith; they say that all that matters is the practical. There are those who have nothing but doctrine, and seem to have no recognition of its bearing on life. In Paul's letters neither of these mistakes is made. In them the doctrine is declared, and then it is applied. That must always be so, I think, in doctrinal preaching. The great doctrines of the faith ought to be preached. But the mere enunciation of a truth is of no value in a sermon, save as it is brought to bear upon life.

Then there is the ethical sermon, which deals almost exclusively with the sanctions of conduct—personal, social, national. The Christian preacher has, or ought to have a national message, certainly a social one, and of course the personal.

Again there are sermons purely devotional in the sanest and best sense, dealing with the secrets of our life, and with the maintenance of the laws of our fellowship with God. Sermons that aim, to use a phrase which is a little hackneyed, at the deepening of our spiritual life. The importance of them cannot be overestimated.

There are also providential sermons, that deal with the government of God, the providence of God, in that sense.

The preacher must recognise at once what is the character of the sermon he is going to prepare. This might be decided in many ways. For instance, a great truth is recognised. It has to be proclaimed, explained, and applied. Or a message is to be delivered to meet a need. Sin demands a message from the preacher; sorrow calls for a message from the preacher; ignorance clamours always for a message from the preacher. The true sermon is always intended to meet a need. The sermon may be argumentative, having an argument on account of doubt. There are always some who are perplexed in faith. The message may be directed to the helping of them and to the solution of their doubts. Or disobedience or some difficulty is calling for a message. These are merely illustrations of different kinds of sermons that we have to preach if we are in the regular pastorate.

The text being found and the purpose defined, it is necessary that the message should be put in form. This means the gathering and classification of materials and the putting of them into such systematic relation that the truth may be presented to an audience. The arrangement must always be kept in mind. That brings us right up to the scheme or plan. Dr. Parkhurst said: "Plan intensifies. Assurance of a purpose makes our work solid and consecutive. Plan centres, energises, as the burning-glass does sunbeams. Shiftlessness is only another name for aimlessness. Purpose directs energy, and purpose makes energy."

I think that is a very helpful statement of the case. I believe that the preparation of the plan is of far more value than the writing of the sermon.

THE CENTRAL MESSAGE 53

The plan represents your thought, the composition represents your expression.

How are we to go about preparing our plan? There are diversities of method. No man can tell another how to make a sermon. Every man must find out by experience the best way of making sermons. Dr. Guthrie, that famous preacher, fastened on a text, and then he put on paper, just as they occurred to him, all thoughts, sentences, illustrations, that seemed pertinent to the subject in hand. Having provided a store of material in that way, he arranged it under appropriate heads, and proceeded to the proper work of composition. Archbishop Magee never looked about him for suggestions, until he sketched the idea of his sermon. I think that is fine. Spurgeon fixed upon a text, and then, for many years, gave it to his secretary, who was a minister, in his great library, saying, "There's my text." Then that minister went through Spurgeon's library, which he had indexed for him, and brought everything that had any bearing on that text, and piled books all round him. He took those books and read all those things, and then made his outline. That was his method. But you cannot make rules for all men.

For years I have made it a very careful and studied rule never to look at a commentary on a text, until I have spent time on the text alone. Get down and sweat over the text yourself. That is my method. Dr. Maclaren thought about the text, without pencil or paper, till he had something to say, and then he went and said it with as little thought of himself as possible. Beecher in his later years never knew until Saturday night what his text for Sunday was going to be. Then he shut himself up alone, and after an hour and a half of undisturbed study on Sunday morning the vision stood before him, and he hastily sketched an outline.

Nevertheless, there are some fundamental matters. In the preparation of the plan there are two processes. Let me describe them as fundamental and final. The first is spade work. The second is done with finer tools. The first prepares for and demands the second. The second demands and perfects the first.

What do I mean when I talk about fundamental or spade work? First of all, we must get ready to begin, by preparing our mind and heart and will. Before we settle down to sermon making, let us be sure that the mind is clear and open. A man is in danger of becoming very technical here, suggesting rules, which are of very little use. Principles are the great things. From my own personal experience, the best hours are the morning hours. For many years I have observed this rule, that when I am at work, preparing either sermons or Bible work of any kind, I never allow myself to open a newspaper until after one o'clock in the day. I urge this upon others. It is good to go to the Bible and study with a clear mind.

There is a very close relation between bodily

THE CENTRAL MESSAGE 55

condition and mental activity. I once heard Dr. W. J. Dawson say: "Half the bad theology in the world is due to suppressed perspiration." There is a great element of truth in it. I think if a preacher is going, to-morrow morning, to get into his work of making a sermon, he will eat his supper with a view to to-morrow morning's sermon. He must see to it that there is nothing to clog the working of his mind. The mind should be clear and open, the heart undivided, and the will yielded and dependent. In other words, we need the constant readjustment of our personal life to the Lord, in Whose Name we are to speak. Part of that preparation may carry us a long way from technical preparation, but without it there is always lacking the very something that makes preaching preaching.

Then, these things being granted, there follows earnest thinking. The text is the sermon, and to that the preacher gives himself in serious thought. It may be that is one of the things most difficult to do, but the habit once acquired, becomes one of the joys of life—real, personal, unbiased thinking. It is so easy, especially when one has built up a library, to look at the text, and then turn around and put the hand on a book. It is a real peril. There must be firsthand thinking, actual work, critical work, on the text. As I said, I have made it a rule never to turn to any commentary or any exegetical work on a text, until I have put in personal, firsthand work on that text alone. Then I take any aid I can, and I find that these aids often help me to correct mistakes I have made. But we have gained enormously if we have first sat down and toiled at the next. This means that, as we do it, we will note illustrations, the pictorial value of words, related stories in the Bible, references that we find. Only let us be very careful of reference Bibles. I am not referring to any particular Bible which is called a reference Bible. All that business of taking a text and looking to see all the other texts indicated is often destructive of real thinking and real Biblical work.

If a man settles down to his work, and makes notes and attends to the words and their idiomatic meanings in the languages in which this text is found, he will be mastering for himself the real meaning and the real intention of his text. Emile Zola once said, when some one asked him about his writing of a novel, that having compiled seventeen hundred pages of notes, his book was finished; he had only to write it. It is the compiling of those pages of notes that constitutes the real preparation for the preaching of a sermon.

I would rather have on my study shelf one book of scholarly exegesis than forty volumes of devotional exposition. Exposition in the sense of devotional application is very, very beautiful, but from the standpoint of sermon-making I would rather have Westcott on John than all the devotional books on that Gospel that I have ever seen.

THE CENTRAL MESSAGE 57

Then comes the final, or constructive work. So far, from the viewpoint of the sermon, everything is chaos. Our business is to produce cosmos, to bring all that mass of material into form. We find our material for our own sake. Perceive it, then reduce it to order and bring out the scheme as clearly as possible. We fashion our material for the sake of presenting it to our people. Prepare for presentation. This is work on the highest level, demanding all the powers of the man. Perception, memory, suggestion, imagination, are all active agencies, by which facts and truths are brought into mental control, while comparison and reason are the means of adapting them to the use of the speaker.

My subject is not psychology, but it is good sometimes just to think of the special faculties that may be employed in this work of preparing a sermon. Break them up in this way. The presentative faculty, the conservative faculty, the reproductive faculty, the representative faculty, the elaborative faculty, the regulative faculty. (I am quoting.) By the presentative is meant the faculty of perception, which needs concentration. By the conservative is meant memory, the holding of the thing. By reproductive is meant the faculty of suggestion and reassembling. By representative is meant the faculty of the imagination. By elaborative is meant the faculty of comparison and of relation between parts. By regulative is meant the faculty of reason and common sense brought to bear upon the whole of the material. We can take more modern terms, but the whole of one's mentality should be concentrated upon this work.

I want to say something about the use of the imagination. That is, in my judgment, the supreme work of preparation. That does seem a most dangerous thing to say—for imagination can play all sorts of tricks with us—unless I add that the activity of imagination must be guarded by the operation of all other faculties. Perception is the grasp of the actual, memory preserves it, suggestion reproduces it, comparison weighs it, reason balances it, imagination sets it all on fire. That is the place for imagination, but if we begin with imagination, without the use of the other faculties, we are always in danger.

May I suggest that you turn to Ruskin, Vol. II of *Modern Painters,* and see what he says on the imaginative faculty. I think you will find it very useful. He speaks of imagination as acting in three ways: imagination penetrative, imagination associative, imagination contemplative. Put these three down and look at them, and use imagination in these three ways, and you will have the whole ground covered.

We should never take any one truth, however great, and make that the only thing we see in our preaching. There is much of that being done today. We always know what some men will preach about next time. They see just one truth—and it

THE CENTRAL MESSAGE 59

is a truth. But if we don't balance the particular truth with other truths, our very truth may become, before we know it, a dangerous heresy. Ruskin also carefully distinguishes between the activity of the imaginative faculty in fancy, and real imagination. He says: "Fancy plays like a squirrel in its circular prison, and is happy; but imagination is a pilgrim on the earth—and her home is in heaven. Shut her from the fields of the celestial mountains—bar her from breathing their lofty, sun-warmed air; and we may as well turn upon her the last bolt of the Tower of Famine, and give the keys to the keeping of the wildest surge that washes Capraja and Gorgona."

What are the essentials of a plan? I have already said, the essentials of the sermon are truth, clarity, and passion. Our thought now has to do with clarity. In order to that we need three things: An introduction, the message itself put into proper form, and a conclusion. Aristotle, in the laws of writing, gives the introduction, proposition, proof, conclusion. In the making of the sermon we don't begin with our introduction or the conclusion. These are the last things. First, the great central message, thought out, systematised, stated. Then we are ready for introduction and conclusion.

First of all we have to remember that there are very few texts which are not capable of more than one sermon. Almost any text will suggest more than one message. I found twelve sermons by

Henry Ward Beecher on one text, delivered over a period of ten years. They were all different; he did not repeat himself at all. He had preached twelve times on that one text. That simply illustrates what I say; there are very many treatments possible, though the text is the same in every case. Therefore it is always necessary to decide on the particular theme that we are going to consider, when we have found our text.

For example, let us take that great text—on which I never dared to attempt a sermon, about which I have talked, and round which I have talked, and to which I have returned—John 3:16. Think for a moment of the variety of tremendous themes that we may find in that great text. God's love for the world: there is a theme in itself, and that text would be a great one for it. Or we may take God's gift, His only begotten Son. We say they are together, but we have two messages there, two entirely different messages. We can find in that text a sermon on the peril of man, suggested by one word, "that whosoever believeth in Him should not *perish*." We can find in that text the great truth, that life is provided only in the Son— "that whosoever believeth in Him should not perish, but have age-abiding life." Life in the Son— a great theme in itself for a message. We can find in that text the condition upon which we may find life—faith in the Son. These are all themes. We may say: "But these are all parts of the one theme. We ought to take them all in when we preach from

THE CENTRAL MESSAGE 61

the text." Try it. There are so many things in it. I have taken it as the supreme illustration of what I mean. Is the whole text to be taken, or one of these parts?

Again, as a general principle, in the message the theme is discussed. In our preaching the work is that of analysis, that is, division, breaking up; then synthesis, that is, the recognition of the unity in our divisions. Here is a danger which often faces us, that we get divisions that look clear-cut and sharp, but when we look at them again they do not synthesise. That shows that we have gone wrong somewhere. One must watch that no one division runs away with the others. If this occurs there is some break in our thinking.

It was the fashion in England, in theological institutions a little while ago, to tell men that the old method of division was out of date, and that the messages should flow smoothly on without any marked division. I feel that that is an entirely false idea. We have a thought in preaching; we want to get our thought over to our people. It is of tremendous importance that we do it clearly, with sequence and relationship. In order to do that, nothing can be more important than division. First of all, to give a clear conception to the preacher himself, so that he knows where he is going. And also it is important to the hearer, that he may catch hold of these divisions, clearly marked. Then, when presently at home that hearer goes over the ground, if the divisions are with him he will remember a great many things that we said, which he would not remember without the divisions.

A little while ago a friend and I heard a sermon. When we got home I said to my friend, "That was a marvellous utterance." He said, "Yes, it really was, but what was it about?" Sometimes you cannot discover the train of thought in a sermon. It may be you will decide it is not worth-while. But there is a way of letting the clear thought grip the people so that they will have your message. I have found this to be of enormous value.

Phillips Brooks said: "The true way to get rid of the boniness of a sermon is not by leaving out the skeleton, but by clothing it with flesh."

I think we have everything there. We should not try to build up the body of the sermon without the skeleton. It is a great advantage when we can see the skeleton—though we must not make that figure go on all fours. Let the people see the bones, the ribs, the great things that form the framework. I am far more concerned about that than about the verbiage. The clothing is important, but secondary.

The character of the divisions depends a great deal upon the text. When a text makes one or two statements clearly, we have our divisions without any difficulty. Sometimes we may make them by declaring the things we are proposing to do with that particular text. Sometimes the divisions are determined by the deductions we propose to make,

THE CENTRAL MESSAGE 63

stating them ahead very clearly, and then working from our text toward them. Sometimes by the applications that we are proposing to make.

Take one or two illustrations. Very reverently again let us take John 3:16. Here are some things that suggest themselves to us, quite simple statements, and not constituting divisions except as we are seeking to deal with them. First, God loved the world. There is a statement which is the statement of the text, but it is not merely that He loves; He has demonstrated His love. Again, God has demonstrated His love with the purpose of calling forth confidence in that love—"Whosoever believeth." And ultimately, of course, He has done this in order to the salvation of those whom He loves, which salvation can only come through their confidence in Him.

Take Jeremiah 31:29-30:

"In those days they shall say no more, The fathers have eaten sour grapes, and the children's teeth are set on edge. But every one shall die for his iniquity: every man that eateth the sour grapes, his teeth shall be set on edge."

Also Ezekiel 18:2-4:

"What mean ye, that ye use this proverb concerning the land of Israel, saying, The fathers have eaten sour grapes, and the children's teeth are set on edge? As I live, saith the Lord Jehovah, ye shall not have occasion any more to use this proverb in Israel. Behold, all souls are Mine; as the soul of the father, so also the soul of the son is Mine: the soul that sinneth, it shall die."

There is a text there—"The fathers have eaten sour grapes, and the children's teeth are set on edge." But if we are going to preach from that text we need at least the other verses. Here is an illustration of the vital relation between the text and the context. How are we going to break up that text? How are we going to state what we are going to do? Let us first consider the history of that proverb. Then let us examine God's answer to that proverb. Then let us state the resultant truths. We have a scheme at once in front of ourselves and our congregation. Once we take that method, several things are in our mind. We have our text, but we must look at the context. When we have done so, there are three divisions. Tell the history of the proverb, and God's answer to it, then we can go on making our deductions. When we do that we shall never preach from that particular text as though it was a truth. We shall start by telling our congregation that it is a lie; it is a proverb that they coined in those days. Preaching from it we must declare that if the teeth are on edge, they have become so after eating sour grapes.

Here is another. "God is love." It is infinite, so you can break it up in a hundred ways. I re-

THE CENTRAL MESSAGE 65

member preaching from it, or trying to. I had only two divisions: "God is love." Therefore His government is perfect. Therefore human wisdom is that of obedience to His government. That is all. It is inadequate, and yet is it? See what it does for you. Behind these two tremendous thoughts you have that greater thought, that God is love. You have a scheme, a message.

I came across an old Puritan sermon which has something in it of the sensational. We think now that they had nothing sensational in those days, but some of them were very sensational, and yet they were very true to the text. John Burgess announced that he would preach on "Beelzebub driving and drowning his Hogs." You know where he went for his text. This is the way he introduced it:

" 'And they besought Him, saying, Send us into the swine, that we may enter into them. And He gave them leave. And the unclean spirits came down, and entered into the swine, and the herd rushed down the steep into the sea, in number about two thousand; and they were drowned in the sea.' In these words the devil verified three old English proverbs, which, as they contain the general drift of my text, shall contain the substance of this ensuing discourse and constitute our divisions. They are: The devil will play at small game rather than none. Second: They run fast when the devil drives. Thirdly: The devil brings his hogs to a fine market."

These were real proverbs current at the time. He proceeded: "The devil will play at small game rather than none at all. 'All the devils besought Him, saying, Send us into the swine.' They run fast when the devil drives. When the unclean spirits entered into the swine, they ran violently. The devil brings his hogs to a fine market. 'Into the sea.'"

That was peculiar, but at any rate it was clear, and I will undertake to say no congregation ever forgot it. They got his divisions.

Let me give you a slightly different one, by another old Puritan. He preached on this text:

> "So Mephibosheth dwelt in Jerusalem; for he did eat continually at the king's table; and was lame on both his feet."

It is a beautiful story about David and his love for Jonathan. He made his divisions in this way:

"My brethren, we see here to-night, first, the doctrine of human depravity—Mephibosheth was lame. Second, the doctrine of total depravity—he was lame on both his feet. Thirdly, the doctrine of justification—he dwelt in Jerusalem. Fourthly, the doctrine of adoption—he sat at the king's table. Fifthly, the doctrine of the perseverence of the saints—he did eat at the king's table continually."

Now, we may read all that into the text; we

THE CENTRAL MESSAGE 67

can make the text the illustration of our doctrine; but it is not really there.

I once heard a man preach on the Good Samaritan. Here were his truths. First of all, he said, the Good Samaritan is a type of Jesus; the wounded man is the type of the sinner; the pouring in of the oil and wine is the type of the Saviour's work; the inn is the type of the Church; he gave him two shillings, which means, "Having food and raiment, be therewith content." That kind of sermon makes me nearly fall from grace.

We must be careful. Take for example the text:

> "Ephraim is joined to his idols; let him alone."

Now this is almost invariably misinterpreted in sermonic literature, as far as I have read it. It is used as a very solemn warning—there comes a moment when a man may be so wedded to his idols that he is abandoned by God. But you cannot study your prophecy of Hosea without having that idea smashed to fragments. May a man be so wedded to his idols that God says, "Let him alone?" I don't think so. Hosea was a prophet of the northern kingdom principally, but he had Judah in mind all the time. At certain points it is as though he sent his voice ringing down from Israel, to whom he was preaching, to Judah. And that is a message to Judah concerning the northern kingdom of Israel. "Ephraim is joined to his idols; let him alone." Make no league with Israel.

Hosea was warning Judah against complicity with Israel. It is still a great text. But it does not mean the other thing at all. To see how far it is from meaning that God abandoned Ephraim, just take another text out of the same prophecy of Hosea. God is speaking: "O Ephraim, how shall I give thee up?" By the time you are at the end of the prophecy, you see in the prophet's vision Ephraim restored. Ephraim in the earlier movements is represented by the prophet as bringing forth fruit, his own fruit. At the end it is said of Ephraim, "From me is Thy fruit found." I mean the whole prophecy denies the right of any man to take that method of treating the text.

Dr. P. T. Forsyth, when he was in the United States some years ago, told me a little incident that greatly amused him. He was staying at a certain seminary, and the professor of homiletics greatly impressed Dr. Forsyth because of a habit he had. On Monday morning he took the homiletic class, and each student gave a resumé of what he had done the previous day. Dr. Forsyth said that the professor said to one student:

"You were preaching last night?"

"Yes, sir, I was preaching."

"What text did you take?"

"I took that text, 'How shall we escape if we neglect so great salvation?'"

"A great text. Tell us how you treated it."

"I didn't try to treat it. I took the two obvious points."

"What are they?"
"First, the greatness of our salvation."
"Very good. What was the second?"
"A little advice on how to escape if we neglect it."

Dr. Forsyth said, "I think there is a great deal of preaching along that line just now." I also am afraid there is.

Let us take some more particular statements of principles. We must decide on our principle of division by having very clearly before our own mind the purpose and the theme. We must have our theme and our purpose in our mind, and then do our best to declare the truth so that it may be clearly understood. If that is our purpose, our divisions will come out of that purpose. Do we want to show the bearing of a truth on life generally, some phase of life, some immediate need? Our divisions will take colour from our intention and our purpose. Is our sermon to be one in which we desire those listening to us to have an apprehension of a great truth, or do we want them to see how it affects life? Our divisions will largely depend upon our purpose.

Let our main divisions be as few as possible. In the process of analysis many subdivisions will be found, but when we get down to prepare our scheme, we shall find that they can generally be grouped under two or three heads. There is the fetish of the three; we must not be bound by it.

Let the divisions be few; let them influence our whole scheme. Never introduce new material into the conclusion. There is a temptation to do it. We have gone through our scheme, we have stated our truths, and we are likely to say something we have not said before. It is a great mistake. If there is something else not pertinent to our immediate theme in our text, note that fact and preserve it, for we may use the same text in that way at another time.

Let our divisions be clearly stated. There again is a point where there may be others who would give other advice. But I think that it is very important so to state them. Clearly stated, our hearers then get hold of our scheme, and they follow us more intelligently. They see where we are going.

Here is an illustration of how not to do it. The divisions are very fine. The text is:

"God is a Spirit, and they that worship Him must worship Him in spirit and in truth."

You see and feel the vastness of that great text. But note this scheme of divisions made by a preacher who said as he started:

"The text naturally divides itself into three parts. First, we have presented to us the transcendental properties of the Divine nature. Secondly, we have the anthropomorphic relations under which those transcendental properties of the Divine nature stand revealed and become appre-

THE CENTRAL MESSAGE 71

hensible. Thirdly, we have the Scripture symbolism by which these relations and mysteries of the transcendental properties of the Divine nature are apprehended, which constitutes worship."

That is like a bad edition of the House that Jack built. The divisions are excellent. He had right ideas. But he immediately put his ideas before the congregation in such language, as I venture to say not one in a hundred would grasp.

Here is a far better example: "Thy word have I hid in my heart that I sin not against Thee." First, the best treasure, "Thy Word." Second, in the best place, "Hid in my heart." Third, for the best purpose, "That I sin not against Thee." The contrast between these two is evident. That is what I mean by clarity of statement.

As to the time to state the divisions, personally, I think at first. I think it is good to tell our congregation just what we are after, and where we are going. State these things as far as possible so as to reveal unity. John Angell James, that great preacher of Birmingham, long ago said: "The divisions should be used for conjunction rather than disjunction."

IV

THE INTRODUCTION AND CONCLUSION

GRANTED the text as such, the theme of the sermon, and the scheme roughly divided into three parts, an introduction, the main body of the message, and the conclusion; granted the message, which is to be the main body of the discourse, and which is systematic in concept and statement; and granted further that the divisions of that sermon are to be marked by three things—clarity, brevity and inclusiveness, let us now consider the matter of introduction and conclusion.

The main body of the discourse being prepared, in order to its delivery, two very important matters require attention: First, introduction, that is, how to call the attention and prepare the mind of the hearers to the consideration of the theme; second, conclusion or application, that is, how to fasten the truth upon the conscience so as to produce the results which it is intended to produce.

First, then, I want to speak of the purpose and of the properties of an introduction.

It goes without saying, but it is important to

INTRODUCTION AND CONCLUSION 73

remember that an introduction must introduce. It must introduce the theme, of course, but it must also sometimes introduce the preacher. He has his text, his theme, his message; his consideration has resolved it into its component parts so that it is ready. Now, how is he to begin? He must introduce his theme generally to his audience before dealing with it particularly.

Someone has said that the introduction to a sermon may be likened to the prelude to a poem, the preface to a book, the portico to a building, or the preamble to the statement of a case in court. The prelude introduces us to a poem, suggests its method and meaning or message. The preface to a book also does that. Of course the preface to a book is always the last thing written. I think that is a justifiable conclusion. The author writes his book as Luke did, beginning with verse 5 of what we call chapter one, and he wrote the first four verses after he had written everything else. That is evident if we look at the tenses in the preface; we see that he was writing it last. It was written to introduce the reader to the subject to be considered.

An introduction, then, must introduce. Sometimes there are obstacles to be overcome. We may feel that there are certain prejudices that we ought to overcome in order that the congregation may come face to face with the message. Those of us who have preached often know what it is to realise that an audience may be prejudiced concerning the preacher. Sometimes the prejudice is in favour of him. Sometimes the audience is prejudiced against the view that they know he holds on general themes; sometimes they favour the view. These are all obstacles. Prejudice in favour is perhaps more dangerous than prejudice against. I do not know that I enjoy anything more than knowing I have a crowd in front of me who do not hold my views. I have a great chance then. Sometimes one has to preach to men who are antagonistic to Christianity to begin with. That puts one on his mettle, and makes him a passionate advocate of his own truth, and that cannot hurt him. It keeps him from all sorts of mistakes. If the audience is entirely in favour of the preacher, then let him beware. He may fall into all sorts of aimlessnesses and carelessnesses.

Another obstacle that often has to be overcome is the ignorance of the congregation. I think one of the greatest volumes on preaching is Dr. Dale's Yale Lectures on the subject. Dr. Dale was a tremendous preacher, of massive type, of great intellect, perhaps the greatest intellect in the Congregational ministry for a hundred years, with the possible exception, on other lines, of Dr. Forsyth. And yet note the simplicity of Dr. Dale's method in this quotation:

"Never be afraid of making your explanation of any truth of fact or duty too simple and elemental. One of the most charming popular preachers and scholars that I ever knew said to me once that he always took it for granted that the people knew nothing about the subject on which he was speaking. A few months ago, in a passage of the great speech on the Eastern question, delivered at Birmingham, Mr. John Bright showed that consciously or unconsciously, he spoke on the same principle. For instance, he explained the precise position of Constantinople on the Bosphorus, and described the Sea of Marmora and the Dardenelles. I did not happen to be in Birmingham when the speech was delivered, and as I was reading it in a railway carriage in the north of England, I wondered whether for once his oratorical instinct had failed him, and whether the audience had shown any signs of irritation while they were listening to this elemental information. When I got home my friends told me that this passage of the speech was listened to with the closest attention. Mr. Bright was right, as usual, and he had given me another illustration, in addition to the innumerable illustrations which he had given me before, of the true method of how to draw audiences. The thoughts of ordinary men on most things not connected with their own profession, are very indifferent. Large numbers of persons who have been accustomed to read the Bible, and to listen to preaching all their lives, have the loosest possible acquaintance with the details of Biblical history, and their concepts of doctrinal truth are extremely vague. They are grateful to any man who will make their knowledge of the external facts of Holy Scripture definite, and who will give sharpness and form to the outlines of their conceptions of truth."

That is a very suggestive paragraph, and applies to the whole sermon, but it is particularly important in the matter of getting your congregation introduced to your theme.

Then, of course, an introduction has as an obstacle the preoccupation of the congregation. The people sitting in front of us may be preoccupied. The best way to know this is to remember how we sometimes have felt when listening to a preacher.

Then there is the attitude of the audience. I don't think we can characterise any audience by a single word, but we do have those in our audience who are patently indifferent. I don't know how it is with other men, but I preach *to* congregations, never *before* them. I see the people. I cannot help it. I am conscious of anybody who is indifferent. I do not look at that person, but half the work of the introduction is to get that person.

What then should be the properties of an introduction? Simplicity, pertinence, and courtesy.

Simplicity. It is good to avoid the superlative arrest, whether there is in the nature of the introductory statement anything tremendously arresting, or whether it is an emotional arrest or volitional, or whether it is in the thought presented, or the language used, or the voice. Some men begin with a crash, a staccato note. Let that be avoided. The probability is that we cannot live up

INTRODUCTION AND CONCLUSION 77

to it all through the sermon. Few men can do so.

Again, the introduction must be characterised by pertinence to the subject. In the introduction the theme should be clearly stated, sometimes by a corrected view of the text. We may know that the popular conception of the text is not the true conception. It is well to introduce it by pointing this out, sometimes by the statement of the theme, or of the text itself in entirely different words, but always as an indication of what is proposed to be done.

Dr. Pattison, who was professor of Homiletics in Rochester for many years, gives this illustration of an introduction and statement of divisions on that very old theme of the prodigal son:

"Doctors take violets to make physics. Preachers take the Lord's stories and make sermons. Well, the process is just the same, stealing the beauty to get the good. One wishes we could keep the violet and have the physics still. One wishes we could keep the story and have the sermon still. I would almost venture to-night to try to enlarge the Lord's story without letting it lose its story form. And I want you to think about what the lad asked for, or what a sin is; where he went, or what a sin does; how he came home, or how that sin is dealt with."

And then he simply told the story, at each point emphasizing the purpose as he had revealed it.

By an introduction the atmosphere should be

created. This depends upon the theme. It is well sometimes to indicate one's conviction of the supreme importance of the particular theme, sometimes to declare its gravity, sometimes to suggest its comfort, sometimes to admit its difficulty. All these things get the audience into attention.

Again the introduction to the message should be characterised, as the message itself, by courtesy. By that I mean, not apology by the preacher for his theme, and certainly not foolish cajoling, but respect for the rights of the crowd, for the fact that the man listening has a right to confront the message with his own thought.

I think we have the finest illustration of the method of introduction in the great discourse that Paul delivered on Mars Hill. How did he begin? Here is one of the little things in that glorious King James Version that I lament immensely, and the Revised Version has corrected it, although they have put the possible alternative in the margin. Paul began:

"Ye men of Athens, I perceive in all things that ye are very religious"—

not "very superstitious." I know the Greek word sometimes bears that translation, but translation should be according to context. He did not say they were a superstitious crowd; he would have lost them. Moreover, it was not improper eulogy; it was a tremendous statement, but full of courtesy. He continued in effect:

"Demonstration is in your altars, and the supreme one is in that pulsing, palpitating altar with its tale of agony, 'To an unknown god.'"

He began on the level of what they were. He knew as well as anyone their faults. But he was courteous.

So much for the introduction. Now as to the conclusion. Here there are two things; the purpose and the method of conclusion.

A conclusion must conclude. And in order to conclude well it must include. In order to conclude perfectly, it must also preclude. When we are concluding we are concluding. We are bringing everything to an end. A conclusion must include the things which have been said, as to their spiritual and moral impact and appeal; and it must preclude the possibility that those who listen may escape from the message, so far as is possible. That means a good deal. Dr. Dale said, in the same volume from which I have already quoted:

"An English preacher of the last generation used to say that he cared very little what he said the first half hour, but he cared a very great deal what he said the last fifteen minutes. I remember reading many years ago an address published to students by Henry Ward Beecher, in which he gave a very striking account of a sermon by Jonathan Edwards. Beecher says that in the elaborated doctrinal part of Jonathan Edwards' sermon the great preacher was only getting his guns into position, but that in his applications he opened fire on the enemy. There are too many of us, I am afraid, who take so much time getting our guns into position that we have to finish without firing a shot. We say that we leave the truth to do its own work. We trust to the hearts and consciences of our hearers to apply it. Depend upon it, gentlemen, this is a great and fatal mistake."

That explains the whole thing. The aim of every sermon is stirring the human will, as I have said before. A discourse which makes no spiritual or moral appeal or demand is not a sermon. Truth is something that must be obeyed. Said our Lord:

> "Sanctify them in the truth; Thy word is truth."

There is a moral and spiritual objective, never to be forgotten by the preacher. Does he preach on "Have faith in God?" What is the use, unless he make a personal application? "Repent ye, for the Kingdom of heaven is at hand." There is no use in showing what repentance is unless the appeal to repent is made. The preacher is not merely interpreting repentance; he is calling men to repent. "God be merciful to me, a sinner." If I merely examine that man and leave it there, and do not lead my congregation to some state of symypathy, I am failing. "Thou hast searched me, O God, and

INTRODUCTION AND CONCLUSION 81

known me." Discuss that as the poetry of a great singer, but until we have made some man or woman inclined to go somewhere and say the same thing, our preaching has not reached its goal. The recognition of this fact from the beginning should fill us as we preach, and prepare for the conclusion.

How important this part of the sermon is I think can hardly be over-stated. Preach for a verdict. It is no use talking morality to the crowd unless we show them it is for them. Too many preachers close with a wrong Biblical note. Too many preachers close sermons that are really powerful in their discussion of moral values and spiritual things by saying:

"But, beloved, we are persuaded better things of you."

The best note is, "Thou art the man." And we have never come to the true climax of preaching until we have left that impression upon our hearers.

A word as to the method of the conclusion. The avenues of approach should be the intellect and the emotions. We are storming the citadel of the will. At the close there should be recapitulation and personal application and elaboration of the truth, intellectually presented. As to emotion, let feelings and brain work together, sometimes by pathos, just as the theme itself is moving us. Never forget that we are storming that central will.

The last sixty seconds are the dynamic seconds in preaching. Of course, it is important not to approach the last sixty seconds until they are really near. If we value our reputation for truthfulness and fair play, don't let us tell our congregation we mean to conclude and then fail to keep our promise. Don't let us say, "Now finally," and presently, "In conclusion," and a little later on, "One word more," and then still later, "And now before we part." Dr. Pattison said that that kind of ending to a sermon reminded him of Pope's ode, with a very different application:

> "Trembling, hoping, lingering, flying,
> O the pain, the bliss of dying."

Don't let us be getting to that sixty seconds until we are there. But let us make that last sixty seconds, as we are able, instinct and intense with all the power of our message.

The whole point of this study is, that we need such introduction as will fasten the attention of our congregation upon our theme; then the sermon in its body; and then the gathering up of everything with the realisation that we are talking to human beings in whom the supreme matter is their own will power, and we are constraining their will toward yielding to the highest and the best.

AFTERWORD

"Preach the Word..."

—*PAUL*

"The supreme work of the Christian minister is the work of preaching"

—*G. CAMPBELL MORGAN*

A GENERATION has passed since Warren Wiersbe first invoked the wisdom of Solomon and called preachers to "walk with the giants": "He that walketh with wise men shall be wise" (Proverbs 13:20).[1] Soon thereafter, as a fledgling preacher, I joined the entourage of G. Campbell Morgan. I have yet to leave his company.

My first preaching professor, John M. Webb, introduced me to Morgan's preaching. Among his colleagues, it was often said of Professor Webb that he grew more as a preacher during his three decades as a professor of homiletics than any preacher they had ever known. Throughout, he made no secret of his admiration for the preaching of G. Campbell Morgan. To those of us who were touched by Professor Webb's passion for preaching it was clear that this was no mere coincidence. Many of us soon found ourselves adding Morgan's books to our libraries. Later, under the tutelage of Dr. Wayne Shaw, I would choose Morgan's preaching as a subject for my seminary thesis. Benefiting from Professor Shaw's background in rhetorical criticism, I developed a more finely tuned appreciation for the preaching of one so aptly dubbed "A Man of the Word"[2] and "Prince of Expositors." Such is the manner in which legacies are born. Morgan's continues to thrive, along with its promise of wisdom for yet another generation of preachers.

This new printing of Morgan's lectures on preaching, which he first delivered as such to the Biblical Seminary in New York in 1925, has called me back to them for the first time in many years. It has been a refreshing experience. Herein Morgan's concise and systematic summary of what he held to be "the essentials of sermonizing" bears powerful testimony to what was the hallmark of his own preaching: *his supreme confidence in the sufficiency of the Bible to convict the hearer of its truth.*

Reflected in His Life and Ministry

This confidence in the Bible's power of conviction was reflected in the whole of his life and ministry. It found root during the formative stages of his spiritual development and was nourished from the core of his personal

AFTERWORD

experience. He referred to his father, a Baptist minister, as "my first Bible teacher,"[3] demonstrated a fascination with preaching even as a child, and was preaching regularly by his teen years. Perhaps most illustrative is the experience, cited by Timothy Warren in his foreword, through which Morgan resolved the doubts born of his encounter with what he referred to as "a materialistic and rationalistic philosophy"—of which he named "Darwin, Huxley, Tyndall, Spencer, Bain" as exemplars. "There came a moment when I was sure of nothing," he said. It is clear from Morgan's own words, cited by Warren, that his victory was the kind born of subjective experience. "That Bible *found* me," is perhaps his most telling phrase.[4]

Morgan's confidence in the Scripture's own "ring of truth" would shape his entire public ministry. He preached through a generation when theological controversies between the "modernists" and "fundamentalists" often became intense, even bitter. Morgan often sought to transcend what he referred to, in 1925, as the "theological controversies blighting our age." He once informed a critic that he had made a resolution in favor of "going on with positive teaching and refusing to be involved in the fight" and, in 1931, he wrote, "I dislike the word *Fundamentalist* as much as I dislike the word *Modernist*. I always decline to be labeled by either designation. My position is that of holding the Evangelical faith in its fullness."[5]

Notwithstanding such comments and his resignation from B.I.O.L.A. in 1928 to protest what he perceived to be the unfair treatment of a colleague by an extreme fundamentalist faction within the school, Morgan's own theological convictions squarely placed him within the fundamentalist camp. In 1921, he wrote:

> As to my theology. In the sense in which the words "Liberal" and "Conservative" are used in that connection, I certainly am a conservative. About that there is no question, as any man who calls himself "Liberal" would tell you if he were talking about me.[6]

As early as 1910, he contributed an essay on the incarnation to The Fundamentals, a series of volumes published in defense of orthodox Christianity against the attacks of modernism and with which the founding of fundamentalism is often associated.[7] While he served as its minister, London's Westminster Chapel became known as the "rallying place for conservative Protestantism" and Morgan as "the rising hope" of conservatives (as opposed to R. J. Campbell, "the idol of theological liberals").[8]

Morgan's response both to the challenges of theological modernism and the broader philosophies which questioned the most fundamental commitments of Christian theism was an unyielding confidence in the sufficiency of Biblical exposition to convict his audience of the Bible's truth. As one of Morgan's contemporaries noted, "He was set for the defence of the Word, not by Apologetics, but by Interpretation."[9] Hughes Oliphant Old rightly calls attention to the humility of the self-educated Morgan who recognized that some of these questions were beyond his abilities and refused to go beyond his capacity to address

AFTERWORD 87

them.[10] However, we should not fail to also notice here Morgan's confidence in the ability of the Bible to "find" others, just as it had "found" him.

However one may choose to evaluate the sufficiency of Morgan's "apologetic by interpretation," there is little doubt that Morgan's preaching did much to strengthen the fundamentalist cause. In almost every case, his pastorates were marked by a sharp increase in attendance. His longest ministries were his two terms at London's Westminster Chapel which, according to David Larsen, "had never filled its twenty-five hundred seats since the new building was dedicated in 1865 but was filled from Morgan's first Sunday twice every Lord's Day."[11] Accounts of his itinerate meetings are replete with incidents of meetings starting hours early simply because seating capacities had reached the limit. Audiences, having already claimed seats, were willing to wait for hours to hear him preach.[12] He served terms as a college president (Chestnut College, Cambridge) and college professor (Bible Institute of Los Angeles, Gordon College in Boston). He would also publish more than seventy books, many of which remain in print and/or continue to circulate through colleges and seminary libraries around the world.

Evident in His Lectures on Preaching

This same confidence in Scripture is plainly manifest in Morgan's Preaching. In preaching, for Morgan, the biblical text is everything. While Morgan's definition of preaching as "the declaration of the grace of God to human need" eloquently captures his view of the essence of preaching, subsequent statements in his first chapter more clearly elucidate his views about the relationship between the sermon and the biblical text. Preaching, Morgan goes on to note, is neither "the proclamation of a theory," "the discussion of a doubt," "speculation," nor "the declaration of negations." Rather, it is "the proclamation of the Word, the truth as the truth has been revealed." What this means for the sermon is made most explicit at the outset of chapter three: "The sermon is the text repeated more fully."

Morgan's three "essentials of sermonizing" (Truth, Clarity, Passion) may also be best understood in this context. A sermon's "truth," according to Morgan, is concomitant with the characteristics of "originality" and "authority." One does well here to pay close attention to what Morgan means by "originality," which, for the sermon, amounts to a kind of transparency. Only God can communicate a truth that is "absolutely new." Originality in man is "always relative" to this divine communication and "he is the most original thinker who is most successful in expounding" God's "two great communications . . . in the book of revelation and the book of nature."[13] Hence, for Morgan: "Originality in preaching consists in the interpretation of revelation." Thus, a sermon is original when it "has in it the originality of the apprehension of the meaning of revealed truth, and of giving it to others that they may apprehend it." The sermon, then, rather than performing traditional rhetorical functions such as "inventing new truths, or even discovering them," aims for a kind of exegetical or expository fidelity which corresponds, in an objective sense, to "a truth already existing and possessed." Thus, for Morgan, the sermon functions to create a kind of transparency through which God's original act of communication may be apprehended by its hearers.

It is from this kind of "originality" that a sermon derives its "authority." For Morgan, a "sermon which is a true interpretation of any part of truth which we have in the Word" possesses both originality (because it is a true interpretation of revelation) and authority (because, as such, it carries the conviction of truth). Whenever a sermon "is an exposition, interpretation and application of some part of the truth, it always carries authority" and when we "preach the truth with that exegesis which means a true exposition of the truth itself . . . that always has the note of authority." Hence Morgan is confident, not only that the preacher is always able to appeal to "an underlying human consciousness" within his hearers but that "the message of the Word on the subject always reaches that underlying consciousness," irregardless of whether it is received with obedience.

Morgan's confidence in Scripture may also been seen as a unifying core around which his other "essentials of sermonizing"—Clarity and Passion—find their significance in triangulation with Truth. Intuitively, one would expect clarity to be a requisite quality for preaching that aims at this kind of transparency and, according to Morgan, "Everything in preaching should be subservient to" Clarity. For him, "making the Word plain" depends "finally upon the Holy Spirit" who can be counted on to cooperate with the work of the preacher when the sermon is true to the will and the Word of God, but it also requires careful attention to clarity of "statement," "diction, illustration and manner of delivery" on the part of the preacher. Similarly, the kind of Passion which serves such preaching cannot consist of an "imitated enthusiasm" manufactured by the preacher and imported into the sermon.[14] Rather, it is that which requires "no conscious effort" on the part of the preacher because it emerges from his own first hand experience with the text: "If he handles his text, he cannot preach at all. But when his text handles him . . . that must create passion." Thus, for Morgan, even the Passion of preaching functions as a kind of transparency through which hearers experience the convicting power of the text and he expressed his confidence that, when accompanied by both Clarity and Passion so conceived, "Truth will always, in my view, make its impression of authority upon the soul . . ."

Consonant with Modern Rhetorical Theories

The convictions about preaching articulated in these lectures clearly reflect, first and foremost, Morgan's personal experiences and theological perspective. However, viewed in historical context, they were also consonant in important ways with the more influential rhetorical theories of his day.

Hughes Oliphant Old, for instance, characterizes the style of Morgan's own preaching: "His English style has no polish, and often his choice of words is disappointing or even clumsy. A master of language he is not . . . One is never

AFTERWORD

impressed with the brilliance of the preacher's words."¹⁵ And of one particular sermon Old notes, "There are a number of places where what our preacher wants to say could be pointed out a bit more neatly. Some of his phrases are frayed and shopworn or just plain trite. Language is not Morgan's strong point."¹⁶ There is no questioning the justness of such portrayals and no good reason to object to Old's apparent attribution of such limitations, at least in part, to a lack of formal education on the part of Morgan whom was "largely self-taught," who "made no pretense of high literary culture," and who thus exemplified the "age of the common man."¹⁷

Nonetheless, the range of sources upon which Morgan draws in these lectures is significant, not only because it includes a broad and diverse array of influential preachers of both past and present, but also because it manifests an acquaintance (either first or second-hand) with classical (i.e., Aristotle's) means of persuasion¹⁸ and the faculty psychology so dominant during the modern age. Viewed from this perspective, these lectures reveal a preacher who was himself a careful and thorough student of the art and practice of preaching. Further, however limited Morgan's own command of the English language may have been, at least one statement in his lectures also suggests an intentional preference for a plain style in preaching. To illustrate the supreme importance he attached to Clarity, Morgan observes:

> I remember when a little book of mine called *Life Problems* was published, many years ago, it was very severely reviewed by a great journal. The

reviewer said: "This man evidently has no use for language other than that of making people know what he wants to say." He went on to say that there were no flowers of speech, no beauty of expression. I pasted it in a book, and I said, "The Lord help me to keep right there." I urge that as something of importance in all preaching.

In all probability, Morgan's preference for a "plain style" reflects both an awareness of where his preaching found its audience as well as the limits of his personal eloquence. However, Morgan states that such a style is "of importance in *all* preaching."

The extent to which Morgan may have been directly familiar with the treatises on rhetoric popular in his day is a difficult to judge. However, he held R. W. Dale, cited more than once in these lectures, in particularly high esteem. During a formative period in his early ministries, Morgan sought Dale out for advice. Their friendship was brief, due to Dale's passing, but his influence upon Morgan was significant and it seems unlikely that Morgan would not have been familiar with his views about preaching. Dale's 1877 Beecher Lectures at Yale (Nine Lectures on Preaching) reflect, to a significant degree, the influence of what Thomas Conley has called the "motivistic" or "operational" notion of rhetoric which dominated both Europe and America during the eighteenth and nineteenth centuries.[19]

During the second half of the nineteenth-century, this notion of rhetoric was notably manifest in two influential treatises which extended the influence of eighteenth-century

AFTERWORD 93

associationist and faculty psychologies: Herbert Spencer's "Philosophy of Style" (which first appeared in Popular Science Monthly, 1852) and Alexander Bain's English Composition and Rhetoric (1866).[20] Whether or not Morgan was familiar with their treatises on rhetoric specifically, we know that he was at least generally acquainted with the works of Spencer and Bain because he included them among his examples of the "materialistic and rationalistic philosophy" which occasioned his period of doubt.[21]

In the end, what is of interest here is that, for whatever reasons, Morgan's lectures on preaching manifest views that are very similar to the "operational" notion of rhetoric so influential in his day. Just as Bain aligned the three basic functions of discourse (informing, persuading, pleasing) with three functions or faculties of the mind (thinking, willing, feeling), so, for Morgan, the preacher "may travel along the line of the emotions" or "approach along the line of the intellect," but "his ultimate citadel is the citadel of the human will."[22] Bain's two most influential previous works, perhaps not so coincidentally, were *The Senses and the Intellect* (1855) and *The Emotions and the Will* (1859).[23]

Morgan's preference for a "plain style" is interesting in this regard. Although some differences exist between the various advocates of "operational" rhetoric, they generally hold that, although figures and tropes have the capacity to affect the emotions and serve the ends of "pathos," a "plain style" is preferred as an aid to understanding. The danger of these same devices of style, in this view, is that they also possess the potential to obscure the associations through which words and ideas are made to correspond. Thus, while persuasion may appeal both through intellect and emotion, and though a rhetor may adopt, as occasion demands, a style appropriate for each, there is nonetheless a hierarchy in the value accorded to various styles, because it is also commonly held that it is necessary (or at least highly desirable) for emotion to be guided by understanding. In other words, clarity trumps all and a "plain style" (usually) best serves the interests of clarity.

Finally, Morgan's lectures also portray the preaching event as possessed of an "asymmetry" similar to that which such treatises attribute to the rhetorical act. In Conley's words, the "operational" notion perceives rhetoric as primarily "affective, a unilateral transaction between an active speaker and a passive listener, between mover and moved."[24] His respect for the right of the listener "to confront the message with his own thought" notwithstanding, the act of preaching, for Morgan, is nothing less than a "demand" for obedience issued from the "Throne of God." He wonders whether, if preaching has failed, it is not because the day has passed when "preaching was a conflict between the preacher and the crowd" and the preacher "was in the presence of the crowd to compel the crowd to submission."[25] The human will is a "citadel" which the sermon attempts to take by "storm." Thus, while preachers may be "talking to human beings in whom the supreme matter is their own will power," preachers are nonetheless "constraining their will toward yielding to the highest and the best."

AFTERWORD 95

In the end, it can be fairly said that Morgan's view of preaching closely resembled, in important ways, the dominant notion of rhetoric in his day, however familiar he may have been with it. That it also squared quite nicely with his theological commitments reminds us that not only did G. Campbell Morgan make a mark upon his times, they also made a mark upon him.

Relevant for the Postmodern Era

With Morgan's lectures on preaching briefly analyzed and contextualized, we are left to inquire of their value for those who preach in our own postmodern era. Of course, the rhetorical situations which confront the postmodern preacher are, in many ways, dramatically different from those which confronted Morgan.

That the rise of new mass media born of technological development has conditioned listeners in ways that create unprecedented challenges for the contemporary preacher has been well documented. The resistance of the postmodern mindset to such dynamics as authority, centralization, efficiency, conformity, homogeneity, rationality and objectivity also generate new constraints upon the means of persuasion available to preachers in many particular cases. A new valuation placed upon the visual, the creative, the expressive, the emotive and the subjective dimensions of human experience have called forth innovation and experimentation in our approaches to the preaching event.

The value of being able to adapt to different situations has long been a staple of rhetorical lore. Yet, perhaps to a degree exceeding any in recent western history, today's preacher is challenged to be flexible in ways that demand competency in multiple modes of discourse that vary in the most significant and fundamental ways. The homiletical literature of the past thirty years has sounded the clarion call to inductive and narrative modes of discourse as alternatives to—or, preferably in this writer's opinion, supplements to—the deductive and linear modes which dominated the modern era. Nonetheless, part of the answer to the new challenges of postmodernism is the reaffirmation of this ancient principle of rhetoric.

Morgan's lectures, however, concern Christian preaching in particular and they remind us of another important part of the answer. Postmodern listeners seek a Word that can impart significance to what they have experienced. It is part of their hunger for the authentic life. Such a Word need not, necessarily, validate their predispositions as to what such experiences mean. It may even challenge them. But if so it must offer in their stead a meaningful interpretation of that experience which imparts significance to it. However one may choose to critique his "operational" views of preaching or his personal theology, that theme which threads its way throughout Morgan's Preaching still offers wisdom in this regard. The supreme work of the Christian minister is still the work of preaching. And our unflagging confidence in Scripture is still what makes preaching Christian. As today's preachers muster their resource to manage the relationship between Word and experience, Morgan reminds us that the Word should always determine the meaning of our experience. Our experience should never determine the meaning of the Word.

I've always considered G. Campbell Morgan's Friday Night Bible School at London's Westminster Chapel a testimony to the timeless wisdom of this dictum. Morgan's new venture was accompanied by the first change in the church's architecture since its completion in 1865: the building of a large circular pulpit, sixteen feet in diameter, behind which was a blackboard large enough and high enough to be seen even in the second gallery.[26] Within two months, Morgan's Friday Night Bible School[27] was averaging an attendance of fourteen to fifteen-hundred[28]—a momentous achievement. If we could, we might ask these people, "Amidst the bustle of such a great metropolis could you not find, on a Friday evening, anything else to do or anywhere else to go? Just what did you flock to Westminster Chapel to see?" And they would tell us, "An awkward looking man, tall and thin—with a piece of chalk in one hand and a Bible in the other."

Dr. Peter Verkruyse
Lincoln, Illinois

Endnotes

1. Warren Wiersbe, *Walking with the Giants: A Minister's Guide to Good Reading and Great Preaching* (Grand Rapids, MI: Baker, 1976), 13.
2. Jill Morgan, *A Man of the Word: Life of G. Campbell Morgan* (1951; reprinted, Grand Rapids, MI: Baker, 1972).

3. Jill Morgan, *Man of the Word*, 192.
4. Jill Morgan, *Man of the Word*, 38-40.
5. Richard, Howard and John Morgan, "G. Campbell Morgan: Preaching in the Shadow of Grace," Preaching Magazine, May-June 2007. 15 May 2007 <http://www.preaching.com/preaching/online/07/May/column_pm.htm>.
6. Jill Morgan, *Man of the Word*, 271.
7. C. T. McIntire, "The Fundamentals," *Evangelical Dictionary of Theology*, ed. by Walter Elwell (Grand Rapids, MI: Baker, 1984), 436.
8. Frederick Webber, *A History of Preaching in Britain and America* (Milwaukee: Northeastern, 1951), 686; E. H. Jeffs, Princes of the Modern Pulpit (Nashville: Cokesbury, 1931), 169.
9. Jill Morgan, *Man of the Word*, 210.
10. Hughes Oliphant Old, *The Reading and Preaching of the Scriptures in the Worship of the Christian Church*, Vol. 6 (Grand Rapids, MI: Eerdmans, 2007), 879.
11. David Larsen, *The Company of Preachers: A History of Biblical Preaching from the Old Testament to the Modern Era* (Grand Rapids, MI: Kregel, 1998), 632.
12. Arthur Katt, "A Rhetorical Analysis of the Preaching of G. Campbell Morgan," Ph.D. dissertation, Indiana University, 1963, p. 71.
13. Here Morgan cites William G. T. Shedd's *Homiletics and Pastoral Theology*, 7ff.
14. One of my personal favorite Morgan quotes is his statement, "Painted fire never burns."
15. Old, *Reading and Preaching of the Scriptures*, 877.
16. Old, *Reading and Preaching of the Scriptures*, 883.
17. Old, *Reading and Preaching of the Scriptures*, 877, 883, 875. Old further remarks that "Morgan's education was strong on the basics, with no frills and certainly no ivy-covered college halls" (876).
18. Among Aristotle's three means of persuasion, Morgan specifically cites *pathos*. His reference to Aristotle's "laws of writing," in which he finds reference to "introduction, proposition, proof, conclusion" is an allusion to Rhetoric, Book 3, Chapter 13 (1414b).
19. Thomas M. Conley, *Rhetoric in the European Tradition* (Chicago: University of Chicago Press, 1990, 1994) 23-24, 144, 152,

AFTERWORD

178-79, 224, 253.

20. As to the specifics of Spencer's and Bain's views of rhetoric, I refer the reader to Conley 250-53.

21. That both treatises attributed to rhetoric an egalitarian import during the same years when Morgan, in Old's words, "was a preacher who exemplified" the "age of the common man" (875) may be mere coincidence but is nonetheless an interesting one.

22. Bain's two previous works, perhaps not so coincidentally, were The Senses and the Intellect (1855) and The Emotions and the Will (1859).

23. Morgan specifically touches on the subject of psychology in his third lecture ("The Central Message") when he represents the various mental faculties as "presentative" (perception), "conservative" (memory), "reproductive" (suggestion and reassembly), "representative" (imagination), "elaborative" (comparison and relation), and "regulative" (reason and common sense). This is, altogether, quite representative of the various divisions of the mind's faculties which, in the wake of the Renaissance, were soon being invoked in treatises on rhetoric to explain the efficacy of persuasive discourse.

24. Conley, *Rhetoric in the European Tradition*, 196.

25. In this regard, Morgan quotes an unnamed speaker at a ministerial conference he had attended.

26. Jill Morgan, *Man of the Word*, 149.

27. The contents of these sessions can be found in The Analyzed Bible.

28. Katt, "A Rhetorical Analysis of the Preaching of G. Campbell Morgan," 48.

APPENDIX

THE WESTMINSTER PULPIT (1)

A Sermon

By Dr. G. Campbell Morgan
(Endnotes by Dr. Kurt I. Johanson)

ON THE WRECK OF THE "TITANIC"

Luke 13:1-5

"Now there were some present at that very season which told Him of the Galileans, whose blood Pilate had mingled with their sacrifices. And he answered and said unto them, 'Think ye that these Galileans were sinners above all the Galileans, because they have suffered these things? I tell you, Nay: but, except ye repent, ye shall all in like manner perish. Or these eighteen, upon whom the tower of Siloam fell, and killed them, think ye that they were offenders

APPENDIX

above all men that dwell in Jerusalem? I tell you, Nay: but ye repent, ye shall all likewise perish."'

And reverently continuing the thought:

> Or those engulfed in the destruction of the *Titanic*,(2) suppose ye they were the greatest sinners on the waters? I tell you, Nay: but except ye repent, ye shall all likewise perish.

The Passage is read, not for exposition, but for service in one application. I must cast myself this morning upon the sympathy and patience, especially of friends from other towns and countries who may be worshipping with us, while as the Minister of this church, and Pastor of this flock of God, I speak of some of the things that are in my mind in the presence of the catastrophe that has plunged the world for a moment into a sense of awe and of sorrow. I think it will be readily understood how this event has appealed to me.

Among the captains of the great ocean liners, Captain Smith was the one man whom I might have ventured to have called my friend. I knew him, I respected him, I loved him. Mr. W.T. Stead for seven years has been a member of this congregation, unknown to very many, he has always worshipped with us, when he has been in London. Mr. Harper,(3) the Pastor of the Baptist Church in Walworth, who is among the missing, was a member of my Ministerial Fraternal; full of hope and joy and confidence meeting with us here on the last occasion of its gathering. Some of the stewards, who names are only names to many, I knew and honored for their faithful and courteous service. Many of those who have gone beneath the waves I knew casually from the fact that I have been privileged to labour in that great land across the sea, which is most sorely bereft. My friends will understand, therefore, how it has been impossible for me to escape from speaking this morning on this matter.

I claim for what I shall say to you nothing in the way of orderly statement, or of reasoned thinking. *Let me say that immediately.* I am too perplexed to think coherently, too amazed to be able to put what I have to say in order. I bring to you the piece of paper which was lain upon my desk, and upon which I have written things as they occurred to me; and here, in the midst of my people I want to talk out of my heart, being almost too overwhelmed to speak at all.

The first thing I desire to say in this House of Prayer, in this Sanctuary of God, is this. Those of us who are Christian men and women need to be very careful what we say about this catastrophe, and how we receive what other people are saying concerning it. Every one of us needs the warning, and the attempted explanation, which I shall venture to sound and suggest at this time.

I want to say, first of all, and so rid my mind of it that I may pass to other matters, that this is not a divine judgment. This is not an act of God. We are to face, of course, with the infinite mystery of the meaning and method of the Divine government at such a time as this, and we are almost compelled to ask ourselves—I am going to speak quite honestly this morning—why did God not interfere? I have no detailed or immediate answer to that enquiry which satisfies my soul. The only answer I have is this: that from everlasting to everlasting He is God; and that His acts are governed, not by the cry or anguish of the moment, but by the necessities of the processes which make for the realization of ultimate purpose. Beyond that I cannot go.

To speak of catastrophe as a judgment of God is entirely to deny the Biblical doctrine of God. To speak of it as an act of God; is to be inaccurate. The iceberg was the act of God; the *Titanic* was the act of man. Nothing, I think, can be more perilous at this hour: nothing can be more wicked, to my thinking; than any attempt to lay the blame for this catastrophe at the doors of any human being. May we be delivered from taking any part in the sensational attempts to blame either the officers or owners or any other. Fault there undoubtedly has been; blame there assuredly is none. The distinction between fault and blame is between ignorance and crime.

Lessons will be learned as a result of this catastrophe which will issue in the salvation of thousands of lives in the course of years to come. That which I am now anxious to impress upon your mind is this, that this appalling event has taken place, not by Divine intervention, but in the process of the working of those laws of nature which we believe to be the thoughts of God. Man in his splendid, his magnificent conflict with, and determination to master, the forces of nature in the interests of his own perpetual programme of progress has been checked, not by God in judgment, but because he has not yet discovered all the laws of nature, he

On The Wreck of the "Titanic" 107

has not yet discovered how to observe those laws, and compel them to his own service.

And now I propose to touch upon a matter which is even more delicate and more difficult to the thinking of some people, and yet it is a point on which I personally have absolute quiet and rest. It is the question of the spiritual life of those people have been involved in sudden and amazing catastrophe; a question that will asked largely by those of the Christian faith whose standpoint and position is known as evangelical; the question of the future of those who were suddenly overtaken, and ushered into the life that lies beyond.

I have already said that here in my own heart finds perfect rest. And in what sense? Let me remind you this morning what the evangelical doctrine is, concerning salvation of a human soul. It is this. No man is ever accepted by God, no man is ever brought into the dwellings of light, because of years of Christian experience or fidelity. To put the matter into one brief sentence, which I think will most certainly explain what I might say at greater length—forgive me if I express it personally—when at last I come to the end of service and of life, whether that shall be by way of lingering illness, or God grant it, by sudden translation, when I stand in the presence of the light and of the King, whether I use the actual words or no, this I am assured, my language will be,

> "Nothing to my hand I bring,
> Simply to the Cross I cling."

APPENDIX

I shall not be received from the present limited life into the larger life because I have been a Minister, because I have preached, because I have loved, because I have struggled after righteousness. To be at home in the presence of God will not be the reward of my fidelity. I shall stand at last in the presence of the throne, accepted in the Beloved.

The light of that fact has flashed for me upon those darks hours verging toward midnight in mid-Atlantic. On the *Titanic* were men undoubtedly whose lives had been godless, men who paid no heed to the laws of God, who had lived in corruption. I do not know them, and I am referring to no persons, but it is more than probable that there were such men. To me it is inconceivable that in those hours these men did not come face to face with eternity, did not realize the grandeur of their own spirit life. And men so awakened are always awakened to the consciousness of sin; and men so awakening, inevitably and invariably cast them-selves upon the mercy of God; and men so casting them-selves upon the mercy are invariably accepted by God. To me there can be no doubt in the matter. I take you back to the old story of the malefactor on the cross by the side of Jesus; only one such story in Holy Writ than no man may be fool enough to presume upon the readjustment of relationships at the end: but one story that no heart be filled with despair. And I believe that when in the light that lies beyond we shall review the thing that has appalled and shaken our hearts to their very centre to-day, we shall discover multitudes who turned to God and were kissed with the kiss of reconciliation, and so found their way of His mercy into light and love of the home that lies beyond.

If we begin to interpret this event in terms of providence we shall tread upon very thorny and difficult ground. I am not denying the providence. The doctrine of Providence is one I hold with all my heart and soul; but I should like to remind you—here again is where many Christian men and women to-day are asking questions, and necessarily so, for who can escape such questions now?—I should like to remind you that the providential activities of God require quantities with which we are not familiar in order to their interpretation. If I do some violence to the context at this moment, I shall resolutely quote the familiar words:

> There's a Divinity that shapes or ends,
> Rough-hew them as we may.

There is a providence watching over the affairs of men, controlling even the choices that are made in human freedom, not to immediate results, but to ultimate and final issues. I say there are quantities and facts and qualities of which we are ignorant, all of which must be taken into account if we are to have an *accurate interpretation* of providential dealings.

Mr. T.W. Stead—how profoundly some of us differed from many of his views, but how perfectly we loved him who knew him best; a man of stormy temperament, fine heroism, magnificent daring, ever true to his own convictions—was on his way with heart filled with delight, like that of boy, to a new enterprise on the other side of the waters, a new appeal to the *men of America to take more definite interest in all matters of religious life.* His body is beneath the waves.

Mr. Harper, to whom I have referred—a man upon whose ministry God has set a seal that is very remarkable as an evangelist—was on his way to Chicago Bible Institute for three months' lecturing, full of hope, full of confidence, full of inspiration. His body lies beneath the water of the Atlantic.

My dearly beloved friend, Mr. Stuart Holden,(4) had his passage booked, his baggage packed. On Tuesday his wife was suddenly seized with illness, compelled to enter a nursing home, and the cable message flashed beneath the Atlantic that cancelled his engagements: and he is in London to-day, who in all human seeming might else have been beneath the waters.

How are we to interpret these things? *It is not for us to attempt interpretation. It is for us to say in the case of W.T Stead and Harper, as is the case of Stuart Holden, God is good,* and often His ways are,

> ... ways which we cannot tell;
> And He hides them deep.
> Like the hidden sleep,
> Of those He loves so well.

There is a surface interpretation which is of value. It is this. For time, Stead and Harper had done their work. For time, Stuart Holden had not. That may not *satisfy your philosophy*, but is it true to biblical revelation. When the heart can find no help by an interpretation of its own wit and wisdom: then we come back to the Bible and say, "*The Lord reigneth.*" "*Shall not the Judge of all the earth do right?*"

I turn for a moment to look at the event in another way. What an hour it was! I am not going to try to *describe* it. We all have a mental picture of it, and those of you who are familiar with ocean travel have a more accurate picture of it than those who are not. An hour of extremity, when all human wit had failed, and all human wisdom was baffled, and beaten! An hour when the sea with silent irony spoke of its mighty power; and the last and most marvelous invention of man for conflict with the sea, with almost human consciousness, shuddered and sank into silence! Now behold human nature; and mark the manifestation of heroism! Mark the loosening of emotions that had been checked and spoiled! See men whom some of you would have shunned, and would not have admitted into your fellowship; nevertheless doing fine and noble things. My heart is full of hope, full of confidence, and I am greatly cheered and encouraged. Panic? Very little, but some assuredly; and yet how little! Mark the story of such as were saved; mark the story of their sacrifices. Read again, and make one startling change in the method of your thinking. I make the affirmation here this morning, that all the things that were fine and noble and splendid, all the things the reading of which may move us to the very centre of our beings, were things which indirectly, if not directly, but not less really, result from the presence in the world of our Christ. "Be British," said the British Captain. And I venture to say that he had to speak for the moment within the necessarily narrow outlook of his own nationality, and yet what it is that makes a Briton admirable under such circumstances? Not his heredity. Trace it back, and you will be very disappointed! But the fact that these Anglo-Saxon people—and I cannot distinguish for the moment as between Britain and America—have come under the influence of our Christ, and the heroism of His sacrifice; and hence arose the ability to cut sacred ties in the interests of all noblest things. These things have resulted from the presence of Christ in human history, and from the influence of the Holy Book of God.

I look again, and hard as it is to say this thing, I feel it must be said; that way of death is a new way of life for many. I have already hinted, and shall only stay to say it a little more fully, yet still quite briefly; that tragedy on the Atlantic will create a new way of life for very many years to come. It is always so. All our safety to-day is the result of someone's dying in the past. In some senses, far off from the infinite tragedy of Calvary, this principle of the Cross obtains everywhere. Let me be graphic and simple. Holborn Viaduct was the result of the dying of Wills of Bristol. Others had been killed, but at least one life, considered, whether rightly or wrongly so, to be of exceptional value, was lost at the cross-ways of Holborn and Farringdon Street. Then the Viaduct was flung up for the saving of life. No life has been lost at that point since. This is a very immediate, local, and near-at-hand illustration.

I said a moment ago we must not apportion blame, but it is high time that we should recognise faults. Much criticism has been offered in view of the fact that neither these liners not the Board of Trade have taken not required lifeboats enough. It is a question I am not capable of discussing in all its bearings, but one thing I have read as an answer given in conversation by one captain of a liner, is worth consideration, "Yes, when you are content to do with less luxury in the interest of more safety, we can carry more boats." A discussion of this matter is not my business here and now. What I do want to say is that as the outcome of this way of death there will be life; and that it is our duty to urge attention, not in any bitter, critical, complaining spirit, but in the interest of human life, that in the hour of such a tragedy as this, life is seen to be equal in value in the pauper and the millionaire, the steerage passenger and the man in the saloon cabin. Human life must be and will be preserved.

Once again, from yet another angle of view. The call of the suffering is a call to immediate help. We thank God at the response that is being given to this appeal through the Lord Mayor's Fund, the newspapers, and the fund in New York. Of course, whenever we give to a fund like this we feel the tragedy of it; as though any financial value could be put upon lives laid down; upon the widowed, bereaved, broken-hearted Southampton to-day, which, if you will forgive me, seems in my thought almost more pathetic than New York; the widows and children of those men, the stewards and the seamen and crew, all the waling sorrow! To imagine for a single moment that we can put upon that sorrow the value of a financial gift is in itself a tragedy. But no one does so imagine! And yet there must be a response. And let me say immediately, for I have one or two other things to say, our offering this morning has been postponed until after I have talked with you, and we shall ask that the offering of the morning and the evening be greatly enlarged, and be devoted toward this fund.

The call of the suffering is to sympathy, to help. Is there a value in it? I do not quite know how far it goes, and I do not for a moment suggest that in my heart I think that it was worthwhile, but seeing that this thing has taken place, is there not a value in it for those men who are giving now of their abundance, and who are brought face to face with the need for such a gift. In the giving which has followed in the train of this emotional awakening throughout the country, in the hearts of men who were in danger of growing hard and callous, is there not a value? And shall not we who love the Lord, pray that while hearts are tender, and emotion is moving anew in the case of some who have not felt it for a long time, that some seed of truth, some call of god, some message of eternity, some sympathy with the compassionate Christ may take possession of their lives! We cannot follow the result of all this; we can only feel and look and hope and wonder and pray. We do realise that this call of the needy for help is in itself a blessing to the community, and an over-ruling of calamity by God for the benefit of humanity itself.

And yet again. What does this calamity say to men? This catastrophe has for the moment halted the entire civilised world, has compelled men toward one line of thought, a line of thought which for the moment, may seem to them to have in it anything of the element of religion. This calamity has inevitably humbled the proud intellect of man. This calamity is telling men that nature is not yet mastered. Twice already I have said it in some connection. I repeat it in this. Nothing more marvellous has ever sailed the sea than the *Titanic*. I need not enlarge upon it; we are conscious of it. The word has passed from lip to lip before she sailed—"Unsinkable!" And we have been discussing it ever since. There is a tragedy in it, an irony in it! There is a terribleness in it, that the unsinkable sank almost more quickly and readily than any boat within recent times. I am not suggesting, indeed I should receive the suggestion with almost hot anger, that God sank the ship in order to teach men that they have not yet mastered nature. But I do say that in the inevitable process men are brought face to face with the fact that even when they were most careful as they thought, even when they set their course below the line of limit that seemed to be the line of safety, something not calculated upon, nor ordinary, happened in the movements of nature, a vast mas of ice floated below the mark; and in a moment all man's cleverness was laughed at by nature, and was destroyed! There, in two miles of water lies the last and the finest product of human ingenuity and skill and thought, with a pressure of two and a half tons to the square inch, crumpled like tissue paper; and humanity is at last halted.

We are not to be defeated by that. Are we to cease building ships? Nay, verily that is not the Divine lesson. Let humanity gather itself again, and recognise that in relation to Deity compels it to new endeavors, to new determination, to new caution, to new skill, and to new enterprise. No one imagines that humanity is called upon in this hour to abandon the building of big ships. There will be finer vessels cross the Atlantic than the *Titanic*, mightier, greater, more splendid; and out of tragedy of this loss of life, and the wailing agony of this sorrow, will come a new care, a new illumination, and a new cautiousness; and thus by this catastrophe man is marching a little nearer to the hour in which he shall be what God intends he shall be, king of the cosmos, master of the forces of nature. But man must climb to that position by travail, by toil, by suffering, by defeat.

Thus upon this whole matter there falls the light of larger values and quantities and qualities of which we know so little; eternal matters and ultimate purposes and great results. I give it to you this morning, as my profound conviction, that even this is part of that process of humanity by which in the economy of God, man moves toward the ultimate crowning, and authority over all the forces of nature that lie beneath him.

But there is one thing more I would say, and only one. The catastrophe that has overtaken the *Titanic* has laid upon all of us an arrest, and a sense of awe. Let us beware in this hour of arrest, and while we this sense of awe is upon the soul, lest we miss the full significance of some of the things I have attempted to say concerning those who have gone beneath the waves, and concerning the place of this happening in the economy of human development. Let us beware lest only short views, and material, arrest our attention.

An hour like this is an hour in which in spite of ourselves, the essential word of all life is heard in the soul. I affirm this morning that though, not in any language which I may use, though not in any language which the Master used, yet in some way hundreds, thousands, tens of thousands, millions of our fellow being have during the past week heard the same message. "Be ye also ready, for in such an hour as ye think not, the Son of Man cometh." "Except ye repent, ye shall all likewise perish."

What did our Lord mean? Except ye repent. Pilate will mingle your blood with sacrifices? By no means! "Except ye repent, ye shall all in like manner perish." What did our Lord mean? Except ye repent, ye the tower of Siloam will fall upon you, and slay you? By no means? "Except ye repent, ye shall all likewise perish." What does our Lord mean? For I will speak of Him in the present and immediate tense. Except ye repent, you also shall be overwhelmed in the waters when the great ship goes down? By no means! What did our Lord mean? Men do not perish by the murdering hand of Pilate; men do not perish by the crushing of the tower of Siloam; men do not perish when the ship strikes the ice, and shudders and plunges and sink to the depths. How do men perish? Men only perish when they live without God, and the way of perishing is the way of refusal to think again, to repent. Except you repent. Except you think of the accidentals of Pilate's murdering, and the falling of the tower, and the sinking of the ship; if you think only in the realm of the material, you will perish. You may perish in your own home; you may perish in your bed, and you may perish in the hour of your dissolution, even when you are ministered to and cared for, and if you have run out the allotted span of human life. In other words our Lord reminded the men who brought Him the story of those whose blood Pilate had mingled with their sacrifices, that these things are the accidentals of life: the essentials are the spiritual. Packed into that word of Jesus is the philosophy expressed in other words that we very often quite together: "Fear not them that kill the body, and have nothing more that they can do." Over fifteen hundred men and women within a few hours buried beneath the waters. And during those hours in this London of ours, how many died? I do not know. I merely ask the question. Do not distinguish between the dying of those in the Atlantic and the dying of those at home. Remember that the essential thing is the spiritual life. There is no judgment there and absence of it here; no mercy here, which was not available there!

So we come back to the word of Jesus. If we allow this great catastrophe to interest us in the matter of naval architecture alone, and to interest us in a great compassion for physical need on the part of those who are left only, to interest us in the material tragedy merely, we are not listening to its voice. The ultimate word is always the spiritual. And as we take our way from this morning's service—which has been one, I know, of pain and strain and tension, and one which one would fain have escaped if possible—let us go, hearing the Master say to us: "Except you repent you shall likewise perish."

ON THE WRECK OF THE "TITANIC" 119

The accidental method of the physical ending of a life is nothing; the supreme and essential fact and matter of urgency in every life is the relation of that life to God. So may we hear this great spiritual word. While we shall turn our attention, and properly so, to all the lessons which we are to learn as to the conserving and making safe of human life; and while we shall, as I do most earnestly hope, give with generosity and even with sacrifice, and care for those who are bereft and left so sad: let us not shut our ears to the voice of the Master, but make this an opportunity for turning to God with true and godly repentance, and yet with loving fear.

Notes

1. G. Campbell Morgan's sermon, "On the Wreck of the Titanic," first appeared in *The Westminster Pulpit V 7 Number 17* on 26 April 1912. It was then published by Hodder & Stoughton (London) in booklet form. Although one of the most significant moments in modern human history, few Christian Sermons, remain in print, on this horrific human tragedy. In 2007, I published, at the urging of Goeffrey W. Bromiley (1915-2009), Karl Barth's Sermon "On The Sinking of the Titanic," in *The Word in This World: Two Sermons by Karl Barth*. Translated by Christopher Asprey. Regent College Publishing, Vancouver, BC, Canada: 2007. This Sermon was delivered while Barth served the Swiss Parish in Safenwil. In 1998, Steven Biel, edited a small volume, *Titanica: The Disaster of the Century*. Professor Biel included, in this collection of essays, poetry,

APPENDIX

and song, a brief chapter titled, "Sermons and Religious Views" (W.W. Norton, NY: 1998). Most notable is the opening, full-length, Sermon by Revd Charles Parkhurst (1842-1933), then Minister at Madison Avenue Presbyterian in NY, on the disaster of the "glittering splendor of a $10,000,000 Casket."

2. Campell Morgan's Sermon was "stenographically reported" and was "printed without material alteration." I,too, have left the grammar, italics, punctuation, and spelling in their original form.

3. In late 1912, John Climie (Glasgow, Scotland), at the request of John Harper's brother, Revd George Harper gathered numerous accounts and testimonies into *John Harper: Man of God*. It was later released, as *John Harper: The Titanic's Last Hero*. The Olive Press, Columbia, SC: 1997. As the R.M.S. Titanic was breaking apart and sinking, John Harper, standing on the main deck, removed his life preserver, and handed to a another passenger. He was heard, until he went "disappeared beneath the waves," pleading with men and women and children, to place their faith, at that very moment, in the Lord Jesus Christ. John Climie includes the haunting line, of 31 May 1911, uttered by a White Star Company executive, "Not even God Himself could sink this ship."

4. Campbell Morgan's friend, John Stuart Holden (1874-1934) in July 1914, two years after The Wreck of the Titanic, and on the eve of WW I in Europe, delivered the Closing Address at the Keswick Convention. This Sermonic Benediction was based on Daniel 3:18, titled "But If Not." In perhaps Holden's finest Sermon, building on Campbell Morgan's discussion of providence, in

the 1912 Titanic Sermon, Holden addressed the doctrine of God's faithfulness and providence. The Sermon is found in *Your Reasonable Service*. Marshall Brothers Publishing House, London: 1921.

www.ingramcontent.com/pod-product-compliance
Lightning Source LLC
Chambersburg PA
CBHW050830160426
43192CB00010B/1968